THE
LINCOLN READING
DICTIONARY

THE
LINCOLN READING
DICTIONARY

HBJ HARCOURT BRACE JOVANOVICH, PUBLISHERS

Orlando   San Diego   Chicago   Dallas

Editor: Christopher Morris

Contributing Editors: Daniel Hammer, Margaret Syverson, Amy Rosen, Gail Rice, Tracy Annis

Illustrators: B. J. Hoopes Ambler, Al Fiorentino, Michael Adams, Helen Davie, Sharron O'Neil

Photo Credits:

airplane: Bettman Archive; **autumn:** Joseph A. DiChello, Jr.; **blanket:** G. Adams/Stock Imagery; **bridge:** Steve Vidler/Leo de Wys, Inc.; **castle:** SEF/Art Resource; **cloud:** National Audubon Society Collection/Photo Researchers; **crow:** A. Schmidecker/FPG; **deer:** National Park Service; **farm:** Harold V. Green/Valan Photos; **fog:** HBJ Photo; **grain:** Frank Wing/HBJ Photo; **helicopter:** Em Ahart/Tom Stack & Associates; **island:** Peter Menzel/Stock, Boston; **king:** Painting by N. C. Wyeth, from the Brandywine River Museum; **lightning:** Viewfinder; **mountain:** Tom Walker/Stock, Boston; **nest:** Painting by John James Audubon, from the National Audubon Society Collection/Photo Researchers; **planet:** NASA; **pollution:** Bob Glaze/Artstreet; **river:** S. Vidler/Leo de Wys, Inc.; **sea:** Colour Library International; **sign:** William E. Ferguson; **snowflake:** Clyde H. Smith/Peter Arnold, Inc.; **sunset:** HBJ Photo; **telescope:** Courtesy of Hale Observatory; **traffic:** HBJ Photo; **waterfall:** HBJ Photo; **windmill:** Christopher Marsh/Bruce Coleman, Inc.

Printed in the United States of America

ISBN 0-15-321129-6

Introduction

The Lincoln Reading Dictionary is a book for students in the primary grades of elementary school. It is intended to be the first true dictionary that a student uses, after the stage of pre-school alphabet books. It is like more advanced dictionaries in that it has a single entry list arranged in alphabetical order, rather than a number of lists of words grouped by meaning. On the other hand, it is tailored specifically for younger students, in that its definitions use very simple vocabulary and elementary concepts.

Entry List: *The Lincoln Reading Dictionary* contains about 2700 words. This total includes about 1500 main entry words, and about 1200 secondary entries that are explained within the main entries. This is a larger number than is usually found in word books for these levels, which typically contain 1200 to 1500 entries. The larger entry list in *The Lincoln Reading Dictionary* is a reflection of the fact that the school curriculum now makes greater demands on students in terms of vocabulary range than it did ten years ago, or even five years ago.

Selection of Entries: Because a dictionary for these levels is limited in the number of entries it can include, there must be a selection process by which some words are given admission to the dictionary, while others are (reluctantly) excluded. For this dictionary, we relied on the HBJ Basic Word List. This is the most complete and most current word list in existence, made up of a selection of 10,000,000 words of running text from over 2,000 documents. It ranks all the words in English according to frequency, beginning with *the, of, and, to* and *a,* and ranging down through terms that appeared only once out of ten million total words in the sample. The entry list in *The Lincoln Reading Dictionary* includes all the relevant terms that occur at least once in every 10,000 words of running text.

Self-Defining Definitions: Any dictionary, regardless of its level, should apply the principle of self-defining definitions. That is, no word should be used in a definition if that word itself does not appear as an entry in the book. This book was thoroughly checked by computer to eliminate all non-entry words from definitions, with the exception of certain obvious proper names and compound words.

Notes on Language: A unique component of this dictionary is its inclusion of special Notes on Language. These Notes appear in colored boxes at the top or bottom of a page. They present explanations and discussions of basic concepts of language, such as nouns, verbs, sentences, alphabetical order, capitalization, and punctuation. The dictionary includes sixty features in all, or about one every other page. They cover all the essential elements of the early-grade language-arts curriculum. (A complete list of the Language Notes appears in the Index on pages 134 and 135.)

THE EDITORS

How to Use This Dictionary

This book is called a **dictionary.** A dictionary is a special book about words. It shows you how words are spelled and what they mean. A dictionary also helps you learn how to use words.

To find words in a dictionary, first you have to know how to use the book. Now, let's see how to use a dictionary.

Entry Words

Entry words are the words found in the dictionary. These words are shown in dark print, **like this.** Each entry word is on the left side of the column. That makes it easier for you to find the word you want to learn about.

Alphabetical Order

Entry words in a dictionary come in a long list. This list is in ABC or **alphabetical order.** That means that the first entry word in the dictionary starts with the letter **A.** The last entry word in the dictionary starts with the letter **Z.** All the other letters of the alphabet come in between A and Z.

All the **A** words are also listed in alphabetical order. That means that words beginning with the two letters **ab-** come before the **ac-** words, and so on. Each letter of the alphabet follows this ABC or alphabetical order.

Guide Words

Guide words help you find other words. Guide words are at the top of most pages. Look at the example below.

dress   **dust**

The guide word **dress** is on the left. That means **dress** is the first entry word on the page. The guide word **dust** is on the right. That means **dust** is the last entry word on the page.

If you wanted to find the entry word **duck,** you would first look at the guide word. **Duck** comes between **dress** and **dust,** so **duck** will be on this page. All the words on the page are in alphabetical order.

Definitions

Each entry word in the dictionary is followed by one or more sentences. These sentences tell you what that entry word means and how it is used. This is called the **definition** of the word. Here is an example.

above When a thing is **above,** it is up high. The stars are **above** us in the sky. Tina has a picture of a horse **above** her bed.

The first sentence tells what **above** means. The other sentences show how the word **above** is used.

Some entry words have more than one meaning. When a word has more than one meaning, each meaning is numbered.

shine 1. To **shine** means to give off light. The sky was blue, and the sun was **shining** brightly. **2.** To **shine** a thing is to make it bright. Paul **shined** his shoes.

Some entry words have other forms of the word. Some of these words tell when something means more than one.

dog A **dog** is an animal. Many people have **dogs** as pets.

Other entry words have forms that show the time when something happened. For example, from the word **act,** which means to do something, you can form the words **acts, acted,** and **acting.** The words **acts** and **acting** mean that something is happening now. The word **acted** means that something has already happened. After the definition of the word **act,** you will see the words **acts, acted,** and **acting** in dark print.

For some words, the sentences in the definitions will show you the different forms.

ask 1. To say that you want something is to **ask.** Tom **asked** his father for a bike. After I finished dinner, I **asked** to leave the table.

Language Notes

On many of the pages of this dictionary, you will find colored boxes with sentences inside. These colored boxes are called **Language Notes.** Language Notes will give you information about words or about things to help you as you write.

> **nouns** Which animals can you see at the zoo? You can see <u>lions</u>, <u>tigers</u>, and <u>elephants</u>. The words <u>lion</u>, <u>tiger</u>, and <u>elephant</u> are the names of animals. These words are called **nouns.** Nouns name things. A **noun** is a word that names a person, animal, place, or thing.

Pictures in the Dictionary

The drawings and photographs in this dictionary are not just pretty pictures. They can often help you understand a word. If you couldn't read the word **squirrel,** you could still find out what it means by looking at the picture below.

squirrel This is the gray squirrel.

When you look at a picture, read the words that are under it. These words tell you more about the entry word.

A a

a b c d e f g h i j k l m n o p q r s t u v w x y z

a **A** means any one person or thing. **A** man came to our house to fix the roof. That TV show is on once **a** week. She has two pets, **a** cat and **a** dog.

able If you are **able** to do a thing, it means you can do it. Tom's leg is better now. He will be **able** to play in the baseball game. A race horse is **able** to run fast.

about **1.** What something says or tells us is what it is **about**. "Where the Wild Things Are" is a story **about** a boy who is the king of some wild animals. **2. About** also means almost or close to. The movie was **about** two hours long.

above When a thing is **above**, it is up high. The stars are **above** us in the sky. Tina has a picture of a horse **above** her bed.

absent **Absent** means not at a place. If you are not in school because you are sick, then you are **absent**.

accident An **accident** is when something happens that was not supposed to happen. I'm sorry I broke your pencil. It was an **accident**. If one car hits another car, that is an **accident**. —**accidents**.

ache If something **aches**, it hurts. Her back **ached** after she had to lift all those heavy boxes. Eddie stayed home from school because he had a **headache**. —**aches, ached, aching**.

across Something that is **across** is over on the other side. My best friend Jimmy lives in the house right **across** the street from mine.

1

act **1.** To **act** is to do something. The teacher told us not to **act** so silly in class.
2. When people **act** in a play, they pretend they are someone else. A person who **acts** in a movie or play is called an **actor** or an **actress**.
—**acts, acted, acting.**

action An **action** is something that happens. **Action verbs** tell how things happen.

actually **Actually** means really. I thought that boy's name was Brian. **Actually,** it's Ryan.

add When you **add,** you put numbers together. If you **add** 2 and 3, the answer is 5. When we put numbers together in this way, it is called **addition.**
—**adds, added, adding.**

address An **address** tells where a place is. All the houses on a street have different **addresses**. The **address** on the letter was 17 Maple Street, Ames, Iowa 50010.

adjective An **adjective** is a kind of word. It tells what a person or thing is like. In the sentence "The little boy has a big dog," "little" and "big" are **adjectives.** They tell more about the words "boy" and "dog."

adult An **adult** is a grown-up person. Your mother and your father are **adults**.

afraid **Afraid** means to feel scared that something bad will happen. My little brother is **afraid** of the dark. He always wants to sleep with a light on.

after **After** means something that comes later. The letter 'B' comes **after** 'A' in the alphabet.

afternoon **Afternoon** is a time in the day. **Afternoon** comes after morning and before night.

again One more time is **again**. I liked the movie so much that I want to see it **again**. You got that one wrong, so try **again**.

---

address Your **address** has two parts. The first part is the name of the street you live on, and the number of your house. The second part is the name of your city and state, plus your ZIP code. Here's an example.

Mr. John Cooper   (Person)
17 Maple Street   (Street)
Ames, Iowa 50010   (City, State, and ZIP code)

against   1. If you are not for a thing, you are **against** it. In soccer you play to win **against** the other team.
2. **Against** means on or close to something. She pushed the desk back **against** the wall.

age   Your **age** is how old you are. Most children in first grade are **age** six. The time when we live now is called the modern **age**.

ago   **Ago** means in the time that happened before. She's not here. She went home about an hour **ago**. George Washington lived over 200 years **ago**.

agree   To **agree** about something means to feel the same way about that thing as someone else. Cathy wants to have pizza for dinner, and I **agree**.
—agrees, agreed, agreeing.

ahead   **Ahead** means in front of. Sue walked **ahead** of the other girls because she knew the way. My older brother is two years **ahead** of me in school. There is only one car on the road **ahead**.

air   You take **air** into your nose and mouth when you breathe. You can feel the **air** when the wind blows, but you can't see it.

airplane   An **airplane** is a thing that flies fast in the air. A motor makes it fly, and two wings hold it up. An **airplane** has a long body where people can sit. People fly in **airplanes** to go to places that are far away.

This jet **airplane** is used by the U.S. Navy.

alike   Things that are the same are **alike**. Michelle didn't know which reading book was hers. All the books looked **alike**.

alive   Anything that is living is **alive**. It takes in food, air, and water. It grows, and it can move.

all   **All** means every one or every thing. I didn't get any cookies. My big brother ate them **all**.

almost   **Almost** means soon or very close. School is **almost** over for the year. There's only one more week to go.

alone **Alone** means to be the only one. Peter was **alone** in his room. He had to study.

along **Along** means from one place to another. They walked **along** the street, looking in the store windows.

alphabet The group of letters we use to write words is the **alphabet**. In our **alphabet**, the letters are A, B, C, D, E, F, G, H, I, J, K, L, M, N, O, P, Q, R, S, T, U, V, W, X, Y, and Z. (See the box on this page.)

already **Already** means by the time a thing happens. Sara is **already** done with her work. She's outside playing.

also **Also** means with another thing, or "too." He ate an apple. He **also** had some milk.

although **Although** means even though. **Although** Jan is not tall, she is a good basketball player.

always **Always** means at all times. Dad **always** picks me up after school. The sun **always** comes up in the east.

am I **am** eight years old. I **am** going on a trip. **Am** is a form of the word IS. You use **am** with the word "I" to tell about yourself.

American Someone born in the United States is an **American**. Something belonging to the United States is also **American**.

among When you are **among** other people, you are in the same group with them. **Among** all the U.S. Presidents, John F. Kennedy is my favorite.

amount The **amount** of something is how much there is of it. One million dollars is a large **amount** of money.

an The word **an** means any one person or thing. Linda ate **an** apple. They live in **an** old house.

alphabetical order The alphabet is the group of letters we use to make words. There are 26 letters in the alphabet.

This dictionary is arranged in the order of the alphabet. On this page of the book, there are words that start with **A.** All the **A** words in the dictionary are listed first, before the **B** words begin.

If the first letter of two words is the same, then the second letter tells the order. On this page, you can see that **AL-** words come before **AM-** words. That's because **L** comes before **M**.

and   **And** means with some other person or thing. Pete **and** Cathy are in the same class. Kim ate some bread **and** butter.

animal   An **animal** is any living thing that is not a plant. Lions, birds, snakes, fish, and insects are all **animals**.

another   One more, other than the first thing, is **another**. That story was really good. Can you read us **another** one?

answer   An **answer** is said when a question is asked. "Where is Karen?" is a question. "She went to the park" is an **answer**. I knew all the **answers** on the test.

ant   An **ant** is a small insect. It can be black or red. Many **ants** live together. They make holes in the ground to live in.

any   **1. Any** means all or each one there is. Our town has a soccer league. **Any** boy or girl who lives in town can play in it. **2. Any** means some. Is there **any** meat left over from dinner?

anybody   **Anybody** means any person. That house is always dark. Does **anybody** live there?

anyone   **Anyone** means the same thing as **anybody**. You may invite **anyone** to the party. Is **anyone** home?

anything   **Anything** means any thing. He ate every bit of food. There wasn't **anything** left on his plate.

anyway   If you do something **anyway**, you do it even though some other thing isn't as it should be. I didn't like the vegetables, but I ate them **anyway**. The water was cold, but he went for a swim **anyway**.

ape   An **ape** is a large animal that is related to the monkey. Gorillas, orangutans, and chimpanzees are kinds of **apes**.

ape An orangutan is a kind of **ape**.

apple An **apple** is a fruit. **Apples** can be red, green, or yellow.

This **apple** tree has flowers and fruit.

are We **are** going to the park. Blue and green **are** colors. **Are** is a form of the word BE. **Are** is used with the words "we," "you," or "they."

area **1.** The space something covers is its **area**. A football field takes up a large **area** of ground. **2.** A place used for a special thing is also called an **area**. After lunch the children can go out to the playground **area**.

aren't **Aren't** is a short way to say or write "are not." **Aren't** you ready yet? It's a holiday and the stores **aren't** open today.

argue To **argue** is to have a fight with words. My brother and I sometimes **argue** about which game to play. When people **argue**, it is called an **argument**. —**argues, argued, arguing.**

arithmetic **Arithmetic** is the study of numbers. When you add, subtract, multiply, or divide, you are using **arithmetic**.

arm Your **arm** is part of your body. Ann carried the kitten in her **arms**.

army An **army** is a group of people who fight together in a war. People who serve in an **army** are called soldiers. —**armies.**

around **1.** When something is on all sides, it is **around**. She drew a circle **around** the right answer on the page. A fence goes **around** our yard. **2. Around** also means near to. I'll stop by your house at **around** six o'clock tonight.

arrow **1.** An **arrow** is a long, straight stick with a pointed end. An **arrow** is shot from a **bow**. **2.** An **arrow** is also a line with a point at the end. The **arrow** on the sign shows the way to go.

6

attention   To be a good student, you need to pay attention in class. To be a good writer, you need to pay attention to the world around you. You can use your five senses to notice how things look, taste, smell, feel, and sound.

A **detail** is a small piece of information. When you write about a person you know, give details about her. What does she look like? How does her voice sound? When you write about a place, give details about that, too. What sounds do you hear there? What smells do you notice? You can learn details like this by paying attention.

art   Doing or making something beautiful is called **art.** Janet drew a pretty picture during her **art** lesson. Painting is a kind of **art.** Stories, music, and dancing are all **arts** too.

artist   A person who makes art is an **artist.** Some **artists** paint or draw pictures, and some make figures from stone or wood. There are many kinds of **artists.**

as   The word **as** means like. While it rained, the sky was dark **as** night. In the race, I wasn't **as** fast **as** Jim.

ask   **1.** To say that you want something is to **ask.** Tom **asked** his father for a bike. After I finished dinner, I **asked** to leave the table. **2.** When you have a question, you **ask** for an answer. The teacher had a spelling question. She **asked** someone in the class to answer it.

asleep   When you are sleeping, you are not awake, you are **asleep.** Brad got into bed, closed his eyes, and fell **asleep.**

at   Nick left **at** six in the morning. The teacher was **at** her desk. Kelly is the best **at** reading in our class.

ate   I **ate** all my vegetables at dinner last night. **Ate** is a form of the word EAT. It tells about something that has already happened.

attention   To pay **attention** is to watch and listen to something very carefully. Pay **attention** when the teacher tells you about a test. (See the box on this page.)

attic   An **attic** is a small room or space at the top of a house. People often store things they don't need to use right away in their **attic.**

aunt   The sister of your mother or your father is your **aunt**. Your uncle's wife is also called your **aunt**.

author   An **author** is a person who writes a story, a play, a poem, or something for a magazine or newspaper. Dr. Seuss is my favorite **author** of children's books.

automobile   An **automobile** is a machine to ride in. It has four wheels and an engine to make it go. It usually has room for a driver and a few other people. A car is an **automobile**.

autumn   **Autumn** is a season of the year. It comes after summer and before winter. **Autumn** is also called FALL. (See the picture on this page.)

awake   If you are **awake** you are not sleeping. Mom fell asleep, but the baby is still **awake**.

away   **1.** When something is **away,** it goes to another place. We scared the birds **away** from the garden. David helped put the dishes **away**.
2. Something that is **away** is far from a place. Alan lives on a farm far **away** from the city.

Autumn, or fall, is the season when the leaves change color in many parts of the United States. This picture was taken in the state of New Hampshire.

B b

a b c d e f g h i j k l m n o p q r s t u v w x y z

baby A **baby** is a young child. As they get older, **babies** learn how to walk and talk.

back 1. The **back** is a part that is behind something. In your body, your **back** is behind your chest and stomach. The boys sat in the **back** seat of the car.
2. **Back** is used to show that something returns, or goes behind. She forgot her money and had to go **back** home to get it. They have a lot of big trees in **back** of their house.
—**backs, backed, backing.**

backward **Backward** means toward the back. Richie looked **backward** over his shoulder. I counted **backward**, "5-4-3-2-1."

bad When something is **bad**, it is wrong or it is not good. Dave feels **bad** because he is sick.

bag A **bag** is used to hold or carry things. Sue brought her lunch to school in a brown paper **bag**.

balance If a thing has **balance**, it can stay in one place without falling over. Some birds can stand by **balancing** on one foot.

ball A **ball** is a round thing that is used to play games and sports. Some sports that use **balls** are basketball, baseball, and soccer.

balloon A **balloon** is a toy. When you blow into a **balloon**, it fills up with air and gets bigger. Some big **balloons** can carry people up into the sky.

banana A **banana** is a kind of fruit. It has a long, curved shape and a yellow skin. You can eat the white part inside.

bank A **bank** is a safe place to keep your money. **Banks** carry on different kinds of business with money. There are also small toy **banks** that you can keep money in at home.

bar **1.** A **bar** is a long, straight piece of something. Chocolate candy often comes in **bars**. **2.** A **bar** is also a place where certain food or drinks are sold. That restaurant has a salad **bar** where you can make your own salad.

baseball **1. Baseball** is a game played by two teams with a bat and ball.
2. The white ball used in this game is also called a **baseball**.

basketball **1. Basketball** is a game. It is played by two teams. The players try to throw a large ball through a metal ring. This ring is called a **basket.**
2. The orange ball used in this game is also called a **basketball**.

bat **1.** A **bat** is a long, round piece of wood or metal. A **bat** is used to hit the ball in baseball.
2. A **bat** is also a small animal that flies at night. A **bat** has a body like a mouse and wings covered with skin.

bath When you take a **bath** you sit in water and wash yourself. The room where you do this is a **bathroom,** and the thing you sit in is called a **bathtub.**

be I will **be** home today if you want to come over to play. **Be** is a special word that has forms such as IS, ARE, AM, and WAS. (See the box on this page.)

beach A beach is a place with sand, next to the ocean or a lake. People like to go to **beaches** to swim in the summer.

bean A **bean** is a food that comes from plants. **Beans** are a kind of vegetable.

the verb be Verbs show that someone is doing something. You run. You learn. You play. You eat. All these are verbs. Verbs like run, play, learn, or eat are **action verbs.** They show that something is happening.
   Not all verbs show that something is happening. Forms of the verb **be** do not show action. They tell who you are, what you look like, how you feel, where you are, and so on. That man is Jason's father. Peas and carrots are vegetables. I am tall. They are happy. She is sick today. We were busy yesterday. These words are all forms of the verb **be**.

bear   A **bear** is a large, strong animal with a heavy body. **Bears** live in the United States, Canada, and other northern parts of the world.

bear   The huge **grizzly bear** is a well-known kind of bear.

beautiful   Something that is **beautiful** is very, very nice to look at or to hear. Those flowers you picked are really **beautiful**.

because   **Because** is used to tell why something happens. He took off his jacket **because** he was too hot with it on.

become   **Become** is used to tell about a change in something. When water freezes, it **becomes** hard and turns to ice. George Washington **became** President of the United States in 1789.

bed   You lie down on a **bed** to sleep at night. A room with a **bed** or **beds** is a **bedroom.**

bee   A **bee** is a yellow and black insect. **Bees** make a sweet food called **honey.** Many **bees** live together in a **hive** or **beehive.**

been   We have **been** living in this house for six years. It's **been** a long time since I saw her. **Been** is a special verb that is a form of the word BE. It is used with other verbs.

before   Something that is **before** has already happened. First grade comes **before** second grade. He ate breakfast **before** he left for school.

begin   **Begin** means that something starts to happen. School **begins** in September and ends in June. It **began** to rain, so they went back into the house. You're not late; the party hasn't **begun** yet. The **beginning** of something is when it starts. We got to the theater just before the **beginning** of the movie.

behind   Something that is **behind** is in the back. She walked down the road with her dog following **behind** her.

better, best Erin is a <u>better</u> runner than Amy is. She can run <u>faster</u> than Amy. But Jackie is the <u>best</u>. She is the <u>fastest</u> runner in our school.

To <u>compare</u> two things means to judge one thing against the other one. You can say one is newer, or better, or more famous than the other. You can also compare one thing to all others. You can say it is the newest, the best, or the most famous of all.

You use **-er** to show that one thing is more than another, as in <u>newer</u>. You use **-est** to show it is the most, as in <u>newest</u>. For a longer word like <u>famous</u>, you use "more" and "most" instead of **-er** and **-est.**

believe If you **believe** a thing, you think that it is true. Jimmy says he saw a bear in the woods, but I don't **believe** him.
—**believes, believed, believing.**

belong If a thing is yours, then it **belongs** to you.

below Something that is **below** another thing is under or lower than it. On page 11, the word <u>bear</u> is **below** the picture.

bend To **bend** means to move in a way that is not straight. I saw a dime and **bent** over to pick it up.
—**bends, bent, bending.**

beside **Beside** means by the side of, or next to. Melissa sat **beside** me at the lunch table.

best Something that is better than all others is the **best**. The Lions have the **best** team in our soccer league.

better Something that is finer than something else is **better**. The first story was good, but the second one was even **better**. (See the box on this page.)

between 1. Something that is **between** is in the middle. I sat **between** my mom and dad. 2. Something that is shared by two is **between**. Luis and I divided the orange **between** us.

beyond **Beyond** is past or on the far side of a place. The lake is just **beyond** those trees there.

bicycle A **bicycle** is something to ride with two wheels. A **bike** is a shorter name for a **bicycle**.

big If something is large, it is **big**. When we moved, we put all our things in a **big** truck. The whale is **bigger** than any other animal. Jerry took the **biggest** apple for himself.

bill 1. A **bill** is a piece of paper that says you have to pay money to someone. We get a telephone **bill** each month for the phone calls we make.
2. A **bill** is also a piece of paper money. Grandpa gave me two five-dollar **bills** for my birthday.

bird A **bird** is an animal that can fly. **Birds** have wings and feathers, and they lay eggs.

birthday Your **birthday** is the day that you were born. Many people have a **birthday** party on that day.

bit A **bit** is a very small thing. He tore the piece of paper into little **bits.** I was a **bit** late and got there just as the movie started.

bite To **bite** means to cut into something with the teeth. Be careful of that dog; he may **bite** you. She **bit** into the apple.
—**bites, bit, bitten, biting.**

black Black is the darkest color. The words on this page are printed in **black.**

blame To **blame** a person is to think he or she did something wrong. Don't **blame** me for that broken window. I didn't do it!

blanket A **blanket** is a large piece of cloth. **Blankets** are used to keep people warm or to cover things.

blanket This Indian woman in South America is making a **blanket** by hand.

block 1. A **block** is small and hard and has six square sides. Children play with **blocks** to build things.
2. A **block** is also a square area between city streets. Mom drove around the **block** twice before she found a parking place.

blood Blood is the red liquid inside our bodies. **Blood** carries food, air, and other important things through the body.

blow When air moves along fast, it **blows**. The wind **blew** hard during the storm. Warm air is **blowing** out of the heater. —**blows, blew, blown, blowing.**

blue **Blue** is a color. On a sunny day, the sky looks **blue**.

board A **board** is a long, flat piece of wood. **Boards** are used to build houses and other things.

boat A **boat** carries people or things across the water. A **boat** moves by using a motor or by the wind blowing on a sail. —**boats** (See the box on this page.)

body Your **body** is your arms, legs, chest, back, head, and all other parts. —**bodies.**

bone A **bone** is a hard, white part inside the body of a person or an animal. —**bones.**

book A **book** is a thing that you read. **Books** have many pages with words printed on them. The pages of a **book** are held together inside a hard cover.

boot A **boot** is a kind of shoe that goes part way up your leg. Keisha wore **boots** to keep her feet dry in the rain.

born When a baby is **born**, it starts to live. My baby sister was **born** just one year ago today.

borrow When you use something for a short time and then give it back, you **borrow** it. Todd **borrowed** my bike to go to the store. Anyone can **borrow** books from the library.

boss A person who tells other people what to do at work is called a **boss**. He wants to leave the office early today, but first he has to ask the **boss** if it's all right. —**bosses.**

boats Look at the word <u>boat</u> in the middle of the page. You can see that there is another word just under it, <u>boats</u>. The word <u>boats</u> is called the **plural** of the word <u>boat</u>. The plural of a word means "more than one" of that thing. That is, <u>boats</u> means "more than one boat."

Now look at the word <u>bone</u>. Can you find the plural of <u>bone</u>? <u>Bones</u> is the plural of <u>bone</u>. It ends with **s**, just like <u>boats</u> does. Can you find the other plurals on this page? Notice how each of these words is spelled. Does every word form the plural in the same way?

breakfast   Look at the word <u>breakfast</u> on this page. You can see that there are two smaller words in it, <u>break</u> and <u>fast</u>. When a word is made up of two smaller words, it is called a **compound** or **compound word.**

In old times, the word <u>fast</u> was used to mean "a time when you do not eat." Breakfast is the first meal of the day. You eat it after you have slept through the night, without any food. So people made up the compound <u>breakfast</u>. It was a way to <u>break</u> the <u>fast</u> of the night before.

both   **Both** means two things together. Keep **both** hands on the bat when you hit the ball. **Both** of my brothers go to Taft High School.

bottle   A **bottle** is used to hold water, juice, and other things to drink. **Bottles** are made of glass or plastic.

bottom   The lowest part of a thing is at the **bottom.** Gary was able to swim down and touch the **bottom** of the pool.

bought   Lin **bought** a book at the school fair yesterday. **Bought** is a form of the word BUY.

box   A **box** is a thing that can hold other things inside it. **A box** has four sides, a bottom, and usually a top. Breakfast cereal comes in **boxes.**

boy   A **boy** is a male child. **Boys** will grow up to be men. Timmy is the tallest **boy** in our class.

brain   The **brain** is a part of the body inside the head. We use our **brains** to think. The **brain** also controls the way we move.

bread   **Bread** is something to eat. It is made from flour, milk, and other things. **Bread** is used to make sandwiches.

break   1. To **break** means to go into pieces. Glass **breaks** when something hard hits it.
2. **Break** also means that a thing is not able to work as it should. My watch is **broken.** It doesn't tell the right time any more. **—breaks, broke, broken, breaking.**

breakfast   **Breakfast** is the food you eat in the morning. It is the first meal of the day. (See the box on this page.)

breath   When you take air into your mouth and nose, you take a **breath.** A good way to relax is to take a few deep **breaths**.

The Golden Gate Bridge is a famous **bridge** over San Francisco Bay.

breathe   To **breathe** is to take air into the body and let it out again. This is called **breathing**. All people and animals have to **breathe** to live.

bridge   A **bridge** goes over water so that people can cross from one side to the other. Some **bridges** go over land to cross a lower place. (See the picture on this page.)

bright   When something has a strong light or color, it is **bright**. The morning sun was so **bright** that it hurt my eyes. The color of a lemon is **bright** yellow.

bring   **Bring** means to take a thing to another place. Dave buys his lunch at school, but Sue **brings** hers from home. You don't have to wear a jacket, but you should **bring** one with you. —**brings, brought, bringing.**

broke   He **broke** open the egg to cook it in the pan. Our car has a **broken** window where a rock hit it. **Broke** and **broken** are forms of the word BREAK.

brother   Your **brother** is a boy or man who has the same mother and father that you have. Lee has two **brothers** and one sister.

brought   I **brought** along a book on the plane trip so that I'd have something to read. **Brought** is a form of the word BRING.

brown   **Brown** is a color. Many people have **brown** eyes and hair. Chocolate candy is **brown**.

brush   A **brush** has a handle and long, thin pieces like hair. A **hairbrush** is used to fix your hair, and a **toothbrush** to take care of your teeth. Paint **brushes** are used to paint a house.

build   To **build** means to make something. The workers are **building** a new house next door to ours. The bird **built** a nest out of grass and string.
—builds, built, building.

building   A place that people live or work in is called a **building**. Houses, schools, stores, and things like them are **buildings**.

burn   **1. Burn** means to be on fire. A big fire was **burning** in the fireplace.
2. Burn means to be hurt by fire or another thing that is very hot. My skin was **burnt** from the bright sun at the beach.
—burns, burned, burnt, burning.

bus   A **bus** is a thing to ride in, like a car but much bigger. **Buses** can take a lot of people.

bush   A **bush** is a kind of plant. A **bush** is like a small tree. Roses, green beans, and blueberries all grow on **bushes**.

business   Work that is done for money is called a **business**. Food stores, clothing stores, and banks are all **businesses**.

busy   When you are **busy**, you have a lot to do. Mom couldn't watch TV with me. She was **busy** working on her computer.

but   The word **but** tells you that something can change what was just said. Eddie wanted to play, **but** he had work to do. (See the box on this page.)

butter   **Butter** is a yellow food. **Butter** is used to cook, and it is put on bread and other foods.

buy   To **buy** means to give money to get something else. Mom went to the store to **buy** some food for dinner.
—buys, bought, buying.

by   **By** means close to a thing, or "near." Emily wanted to sit **by** her friend Jennie on the bus.

---

but   Notice the words <u>and</u> and <u>but</u> in these sentences. "Heather likes to play soccer, <u>but</u> her brother doesn't. He likes to play baseball <u>and</u> basketball."

    The word <u>but</u> is called a **conjunction**. <u>And</u> is a **conjunction** too. A **conjunction** joins things together. It joins two ideas in the same sentence. Notice that <u>and</u> joins two ideas that are like each other. He likes baseball <u>and</u> basketball. <u>But</u> joins two ideas that are different from each other. Heather likes to play soccer, <u>but</u> her brother doesn't.

C c

a b C d e f g h i j k l m n o p q r s t u v w x y z

cake   **Cake** is something to eat. **Cakes** are made of flour, butter, eggs, sugar, and other things. People eat **cake** for dessert.

calendar   A **calendar** shows the month, week, and day. Cara looked at her **calendar** to see what day of the week her birthday came on this year.

call   **1.** To say something in a loud voice is to **call**. I **called** the dog to get him to come in from the back yard.
2. Call means to use a name for someone. My name is James, but my friends **call** me Jimmie.
3. When you use the telephone, you **call** someone. We always **call** Grandma on her birthday.

came   My cousin Lisa **came** to visit us last summer. **Came** is a form of the word COME.

camera   A **camera** is a small machine used to take pictures or make movies. You look through a small window on the **camera** to take a picture. What you see in the window is then copied on FILM inside the **camera**.

camp   A **camp** is a place away from cities where people live outside for a short time. My family goes **camping** for a few weeks each summer.

can   When you know how or are able to do something, you **can** do it. Birds **can** fly. I **can** name all fifty states.

can   A **can** is something that holds other things. Most **cans** are round at the top and made of metal. Chris opened a **can** of soup for his lunch. Please put these papers in the garbage **can**.

candy **Candy** is something that tastes good to eat. It is made of sugar and is sweet.

cannot When you **cannot** do something, you don't know how to do it or are not able to do it. Cats can climb trees, but dogs **cannot**.

can't **Can't** is a short way to say or write CANNOT. He's just a little baby and **can't** talk yet.

capital **1.** The **capital** of a country or a state is the place where the government meets. The city of Washington, D.C. is the **capital** of the United States **2.** A **capital letter** is a tall letter. These letters are **capitals**: A B C. These letters are small: a b c. (See the box on this page.)

car A **car** is something you ride in. A **car** has four wheels, seats, windows, and an engine to make it go. The roads are made for **cars** to travel on.

card A **card** is a piece of thick paper. Most **cards** have writing or pictures on them. Grandpa sent me a **card** for my birthday. Special kinds of **cards** are used to play games.

care When you **care**, it means you are worried or thinking a lot about something. Mom says I can get a dog for a pet if I take good **care** of it myself.

careful When you are **careful**, you watch what you are doing so you don't make a mistake. Dad always tells us to be **careful** when we cross the street. If you don't think about what you're doing, you are **careless.** He was **careless** with his paper and left out a lot of words.

carry **Carry** means to hold a thing and move it to another place. The mother **carried** the baby in her arms. A school bus can **carry** a lot of people. —**carries, carried, carrying.**

capital letters The word **capital** means something big or important. A city that is the capital of a country is a big, important city. A **capital letter** is a bigger letter used to show that a certain word is important.

Capital letters are used for: (1) The first word in a sentence: **T**he teacher is not here. **S**he is sick today. (2) The name of a person, place, or thing: **M**ary **S**mith, **D**allas, **T**exas, **S**upreme **C**ourt. (3) The title of a book: **T**he **T**ime **M**achine, **H**ow **P**lants **G**row. (4) The title of a person: **D**r. **J**ones, **M**rs. **R**oss. (5) The word **I**: Why can't **I** go to the movies?

19

case 1. A thing that covers or holds another thing is a **case**. The store keeps its cameras inside a glass **case**. Catherine has a new **bookcase** in her bedroom.
2. A **case** is an example of something. In **case** of rain, the game will not be played.

cash **Cash** is money in the form of coins and bills. Dad had to pay for the pizza with a check, because he didn't have any **cash** with him.

castle A **castle** is a very big building that was built long ago. **Castles** are made of stone. Kings and queens lived in **castles**.

castle This famous **castle** in the country of Spain is almost 1000 years old.

cat A **cat** is an animal. **Cats** have soft hair, four legs, and a long tail. Many people have **cats** as pets. Lions and tigers are also part of the **cat** family.

catch **Catch** means to take hold of a thing that is moving. In baseball you try to **catch** the ball. My sister **caught** a big fish in the lake last week.
—**catches, caught, catching.**

cause To **cause** something is to make it happen. Playing with matches can **cause** a fire.

cave A **cave** is a hole in the side of a hill or mountain. Bears sometimes live in **caves**.

ceiling The **ceiling** is the top part of a room, above the walls.

cellar A **cellar** is the bottom part of a house, under the ground. A **cellar** is also called a **basement**.

cent A **cent** is a piece of money. One **penny** is a **cent**. A **nickel** is worth five **cents,** and a **dime** is ten **cents**.

center The **center** of something is the middle. The boy who was 'it' got in the **center** and we all made a circle around him.

changes in a word   In this dictionary, we list each entry word in heavy black letters. For example, you can see on this page **chair** and **change**. But if you look at those words you will also see other words in black, such as **chairs** and **changed.**

Those words look like the entry words, but there is a difference. **Chairs** means more than one chair. **Changed** shows an action that happened in the past. Words change by adding letters at the end, such as **s** or **ed**. But the real meaning of the word stays the same.

cereal **Cereal** is a kind of food. It is made from wheat, corn, rice, or something like that. People eat **cereal** for breakfast.

certain   1. When you are very sure of something, you are **certain**. Rachel made **certain** that her little brother stayed right near her at the park.
2. **Certain** is also used to show the thing talked about. **Certain** trees do not lose their leaves in winter.
3. **Certainly** also means that something is sure. It **certainly** is hot out there today. It must be at least 90.

chain A **chain** is a row of metal rings that are joined together. I keep my dog on a **chain** when I take him for a walk. A bike has a **chain** to make the wheels go.

chair A **chair** is a thing that you can sit on. Most **chairs** have four legs and a back.

chance   1. A **chance** is a time to do something. Most of the time a **chance** happens by luck, or as a surprise. My older sister got a **chance** to be on television.
2. A **chance** is also a time when something might happen. There is a **chance** it could rain today. They have a really good team. **Chances** are they'll win the game today.

change   1. A thing that **changes** is not the same as it was before. In the fall the leaves **change** color. After school Stacey **changed** into her play clothes. (See the box on this page.)
2. **Change** also means money. The newspaper cost 25 cents. I gave him a dollar and got 75 cents **change**.

channel   On a television set there are numbers for each of the different **channels**. The **channel** tells you where to find a certain show you want to watch.

charge   **1.** The amount of money that you have to pay for something is the **charge**. The **charge** to get into the movie was five dollars. They **charged** fifty dollars to cut down our old tree. **2.** When you **charge** something you buy it but pay for it later. Stores often let people **charge** the things they buy.
—**charges, charged, charging.**

chase   **Chase** means to run and try to catch something. When I throw the ball, my dog **chases** it.

cheap   Something that is **cheap** does not cost much money. This shirt cost only five dollars. That's really **cheap**.

check   **1.** When you make sure something is right, you **check** it. Bob **checked** his pocket to make sure he had his money. **2.** A mark that is made next to something to show that it was **checked** is called a **check**. A **check** looks like this: √ **3.** A **check** is a piece of paper that is used in place of money to pay for something.
—**checks, checked, checking.**

cheese   **Cheese** is a kind of food made from milk. There are many different kinds of **cheese**.

cherry   A **cherry** is a fruit that we eat. **Cherries** grow on trees. They are small, round, and red.

This is a **cherry** tree, with its fruit shown in front.

chest   **1.** Your **chest** is the part of your body that is below your neck and above your stomach. Your heart is in your **chest**. **2.** A **chest** is also a big box made of metal or wood. Danny keeps his toys in a toy **chest**.

chew   **Chew** means to cut things with the teeth. Kevin **chewed** his food carefully. The dog was **chewing** on a bone.

chicken A **chicken** is a bird. People eat meat from **chickens**. They also eat **chickens'** eggs.

chief A **chief** is the head of a group of people. The **chief** of police tells the policemen what to do. An Indian **chief** is the leader of a group of Indians.

child A **child** is a boy or girl. **Children** means more than one **child.** All **children** must go to school.

chocolate **Chocolate** is a food to eat for dessert or as a snack. It is brown and sweet. **Chocolate** is used in candy or to make ice cream and cookies.

choose When you pick out one thing from other things, you **choose** it. Mom let me **choose** what I wanted to have for lunch. The soccer coach **chose** Nikki to be the goalie for the game today. (See the box on this page.)

Christmas **Christmas** is a holiday for the day Jesus Christ was born. It is on December 25th. People give each other presents on **Christmas**.

church A **church** is a special kind of building. People go to **church** to show love for God.

circle A **circle** is a round shape, like this. O A wheel and a ring are **circles.**

circus A **circus** is a kind of show. It has people and animals that do many different tricks.

city A **city** is a very big place where many people live and work. **Cities** have tall buildings and are busy places. New York is a famous American **city.**

class The children in the same room at school are a **class.** In this school, there are four different **classes** in first grade.

---

choosing the right word Teachers say, "Choose the right word when you write." What do they mean? What is the right word?

Jimmy wrote "Maria saw happy." But you can't "see" that way. He meant to write was instead of saw, and got the letters mixed up. He should check his work to be sure he chose the right way to spell a word.

"I moved the ball to Maria." But moved is not the right word. Did he throw it? Kick it? Hit it? Jimmy should think about what he is writing. He should choose the word that best tells what he did.

23

clean   A thing that is **clean** does not have dirt on it. You wash something to make it **clean**. Andy **cleaned** his room before he went out to play.
—**cleans, cleaned, cleaning.**

clear   Something that is **clear** is easy to see through. Glass for windows is **clear**. On a **clear** day, the sun is bright and you can see a long way.

climb   To **climb** means to use your hands and feet to go up. The cat **climbed** the tree.

clock   A **clock** tells you what time it is. Some **clocks** have hands that point to the time. Other **clocks** tell the time with numbers.

close   You **close** something when you shut it. A thing that is **closed** is not open. It's cold in here. Please **close** that window.
—**closes, closed, closing.**

close   A thing that is **close** is near by, not far away. My house is **close** to school and I can walk there.

closet   A **closet** is a place in a room where clothes and other things are kept.

cloth   **Cloth** is what clothes are made of. **Cloth** is also used to make other things such as rugs and blankets.

clothes   **Clothes** are things to wear. Shirts, pants, dresses, and coats are all **clothes**. These things are also called **clothing.**

cloud   A **cloud** is a thing in the sky made of little drops of water. Dark **clouds** can mean that rain is coming.

This big white **cloud** is a storm cloud.

clown   A **clown** is a person who does tricks or tells jokes to make you laugh. **Clowns** usually wear funny clothes and paint their faces with bright colors.

coach   A **coach** is a person who tells a sports team what to do. The players on a football team have to do what the **coach** says.

coat A **coat** is something you wear over other clothes to keep you warm. In winter I wear a heavy **coat** to school.
—**coats.**

coffee **Coffee** is a hot, dark-brown drink. My mom has a cup of **coffee** when she gets up in the morning.

coin A **coin** is a flat, round piece of money. **Coins** are made of metal. Quarters, dimes, nickels, and pennies are **coins**.

cold **1.** When something is not hot, it is **cold**. Ice and snow are **cold**. In winter the water in the ocean is **cold**.
2. A **cold** is a name for a certain way of being sick. People often get **colds** in the winter.

collect To **collect** things means to put them together and keep them. Andrew likes to **collect** baseball cards. The teacher **collected** two dollars from each of us to pay for the class trip.
—**collects, collected, collecting.**

college A **college** is a place where people go to learn after they get out of high school. **Colleges** have places for people to live while they go there.

color A **color** is the way that something looks when light is on it. Red, yellow, and blue are **colors**. Grass has a green **color**.

comb A **comb** is a thing you use to make your hair look nice.

come **1.** When you go or move to a place, you **come**. I'm going to the park to play. Do you want to **come** with me? My grandma **came** to see us last weekend.
2. When something happens, it **comes**. Your birthday **comes** on the same day each year.
—**comes, came, coming.**

commercial On television or radio, a **commercial** tries to get you to buy something. Many children's shows on TV have **commercials** for different toys.

common If a thing is **common,** you see it or hear of it a lot. "Smith" is a **common** last name that many people have.

company **1.** A **company** is a special group of people who work together. The Ford Motor **Company** makes and sells cars.
2. Company is also someone who comes to visit. We're having **company** today. My Uncle Don is coming to dinner.

contractions   "Cats <u>do not</u> like the water. Dogs like to swim, but cats <u>don't</u>." The two words <u>do not</u> and the one word <u>don't</u> mean the same thing. <u>Don't</u> is just a shorter way to say or write "do not."

The word <u>don't</u> is a **contraction.** A contraction puts two words together to make one word. A contraction is formed by taking one or more letters out of the second word. There are contractions for words that we use all the time. <u>It is</u> can also be <u>it's</u>. <u>She is</u> can also be <u>she's</u>. <u>They are</u> can also be <u>they're</u>. <u>I am</u> can be <u>I'm</u>. <u>Will not</u> can be <u>won't</u>.

complete   1. If you **complete** something, it means you finish it. The teacher said that we had one hour to **complete** the test. 2. A thing is **complete** when all of it is there. They are going to show the **complete** movie on TV. No parts have been cut out.

computer   A **computer** is a machine that is used to keep a lot of information. **Computers** can tell you information very quickly. Stores use **computers** to help them in business. Other kinds of **computers** are used to play games.

contest   A **contest** is a race or a game between two or more people. You try to win a **contest**. Our class had a **contest** to see who could read the most books.

continue   To **continue** is to keep on doing something. It started snowing in the afternoon and **continued** to snow all night.

control   To **control** something is to make it do what you want it to. The driver of a car **controls** the way the car moves.

cook   **Cooking** means making food ready to eat. To **cook** food, you make it hot. My mom is a good **cook** and I like the meals she makes.
—**cooks, cooked, cooking.**

cookie   A **cookie** is a little sweet food. People eat **cookies** as a snack or for dessert.

cool   Something is **cool** when it is a little cold. In the early fall, we often have **cool** days here.

copy   To **copy** means to make or do something that is just like another thing. I read the list of words in the book and **copied** them down on my paper. This machine can make a **copy** of your letter for you to keep.
—**copies, copied, copying.**

corn   **Corn** is a kind of food. It is a yellow vegetable that grows on a very tall green plant.

corner   A **corner** is the place where two things meet. The bank is at the **corner** of Third Street and Milton Road.

correct   **Correct** means "right." When a thing is done as it should be, it is **correct**. If you say, "How much is 2 and 2?" the **correct** answer is "4." I got the wrong answer, and the teacher **corrected** me.

cost   The **cost** is what you have to pay for a thing. It **costs** fifty cents to ride the bus. How much does this book **cost**?

costume   A **costume** is special clothes you wear when you dress up as someone else.

Children wear **costumes** on Halloween.

cough   You **cough** when you move air out of your mouth in a sudden, noisy way. People often **cough** when they have a cold.

could   If you **could** ride a bike when you were five, it means that you were able to do it then. **Could** is a form of CAN. It is used to tell about something that has already happened.

couldn't   **Couldn't** is a short way to write or say "could not."

count   When you **count,** you find out how many things there are. Tim **counted** all the rocks he picked up on the beach and found out there were 21.

country   1. A **country** is a large area of land and all the people who live in it. Our **country** is the United States. There are many other **countries** in the world.
2. The **country** is a place that is away from big cities and towns. The **country** has a lot of open land with no buildings.

couple   1. A **couple** is two people together. A man and woman who are married are a **couple.**
2. **Couple** also means "about two or three." I sent the letter today, so he'll get it in a **couple** of days.

course **Of course** is another way to say "Yes" or "That's right." He asked, "You like ice cream, don't you?" I said, "**Of course** I do. I love ice cream."

cousin A child of your aunt and uncle is your **cousin.**
—**cousins.**

cover To **cover** a thing means to put something over it. The noise was so loud that I **covered** my ears with my hands. We had to put paper **covers** on all our school books.
—**covers, covered, covering.**

cow A **cow** is a large farm animal. **Cows** give milk and are used for meat. The male of this animal is a **bull.** Cows and bulls together are called **cattle.**

crack A **crack** is a small break in a thing. The car window had a **crack** in it where a stone hit it. The glass **cracked** when I dropped it into the sink.
—**cracks, cracked, cracking.**

crash A **crash** is a loud noise. He dropped the dishes and they **crashed** to the floor.
2. When an airplane falls and hits the ground, that is a **crash.**
—**crashes, crashed, crashing.**

crawl To **crawl** means to move on your hands and knees. Little babies **crawl** along the floor before they learn to walk.

cream **Cream** is a food made from the thick part of milk. **Cream** is used to make **butter.**

crooked Something **crooked** is not straight. A **crooked** road has lots of turns and curves.

cross To **cross** means to go from one side to the other. I have to **cross** Miller Street on my way to school.
—**crosses, crossed, crossing.**

crow A **crow** is a kind of bird. **Crows** have black feathers and a loud, rough voice.

The **crow** is often seen in open fields.

curious   The word **curious** means that you want to know something. You want to find out "why" or "how" or "where." Have you ever been <u>curious</u> about where our words come from?

The word <u>curious</u> comes from another language, French. Hundreds of years ago, English people heard French people use this word. They "borrowed" the word to use in their own language. <u>Curious</u> comes from a French word that means "care." The idea is that if you care about something, you will want to find out more about it.

crowd   A lot of people together is a **crowd**. When the store had a sale, a big **crowd** of people came to buy things. They **crowded** around the doors, waiting for the store to open.
—crowds, crowded, crowding.

cry   People may **cry** when they feel very bad about something. When you **cry,** a kind of water called **tears** comes from your eyes. Billy **cried** when he fell off his bike and hurt his leg.
—cries, cried, crying.

cube   A **cube** is a shape with six sides that are the same size. Toy blocks are **cubes**.

cup   1. A **cup** is something you drink from. It is usually smaller than a glass, and it is not made so that you can see through it.
2. A **cup** is a way to measure how much there is of a thing. Jamie used six **cups** of water when she made the soup.

curious   If you are **curious**, you want to know about things. Elise was **curious** about dinosaurs, so she read a book about them. (See the box on this page.)

curl   Hair that **curls** turns around itself in circles or rings. My sister's hair is very **curly**.

curve   A **curve** is a round part. It can look like part of a circle. (The sign shows that the road **curves** to the right up ahead.

cut   If you **cut** something, you move a knife or another sharp thing into it. She **cut** the meat into small pieces. I **cut** my foot when I stepped on the broken glass. Dave's hair is getting long. He needs a **haircut**.
—cuts, cut, cutting.

cute   **Cute** means that a thing looks nice and pretty. My baby sister looks so **cute** when she is sleeping.

D d

a b c **d** e f g h i j k l m n o p q r s t u v w x y z

daily   When a thing happens **daily,** it happens every day. A **daily** newspaper comes out every day of the week.

damp   When a thing is **damp**, it is still a little bit wet. The clothes I put out to dry were still **damp**.

dance   To **dance** is to move your body when you listen to music. When you do this, it is called **dancing.** My older sister went to a **dance** at her high school.

danger   **Danger** means that something could hurt you. A person who drives a car too fast is in **danger** of having an accident.

dark   When something is **dark**, it is not light. When the sun goes down, the sky gets **dark**. Black is a **dark** color.

date   The **date** tells what day, month, and year it is. February 12, 1809 is the **date** President Abraham Lincoln was born.

daughter   A girl or woman is the **daughter** of her mother and father.
—**daughters**.

dawn   **Dawn** is the first light of day, when the sun comes up in the morning.

day   1. **Day** is when it is light outside. **Day** is the time when it is not night.
2. **Day** also means a time of one complete day and night. A **day** has 24 hours. There are 7 **days** in a week.

dead   If something is **dead,** it is no longer alive. This is called **death.**

dear   1. When you write a letter, you start with the word "**dear**." Laura wrote a letter to her aunt that began "**Dear** Aunt Karen." 2. When you say someone is **dear**, it means you care a lot about that person.

decide   **Decide** means to make up your mind to do something. He **decided** to buy the blue shirt because the red one was too big.

deep   Something is **deep** when it goes far down. The water of the Pacific Ocean is very **deep**.

deer   A **deer** is a large animal that can run very fast. Many **deer** live in the woods.

This animal is called a mule **deer**.

delicious   Something that is **delicious** has a very good taste. That chicken dinner was really **delicious**.

dentist   A **dentist** is a kind of doctor who takes care of people's teeth.

department   A **department** is a special part of something. The Fire **Department** puts out fires. This store sells toys and games in the Toy **Department.**

desert   A **desert** is a very dry place that has almost no rain. Sand covers the ground and not many plants can grow there. It gets very hot in the **desert**.

design   The **design** of a thing is the way it looks. That car has a beautiful **design.** Their house is **designed** so that the bedrooms are all on the second floor.

desk   A **desk** is a kind of table that you sit at to write or read. Students in school and people who work in offices have **desks.**

dessert   **Dessert** is sweet food eaten at the end of a meal. Pie and ice cream are **desserts**.

diamond   1. A **diamond** is a very hard stone that is clear like glass. **Diamonds** cost a lot of money.
2. A **diamond** is also a shape. It looks like this. ◊

31

dictionary   This book you are reading now is called a **dictionary**. A dictionary is a book of words. The words in a dictionary come in a long list. The list starts at **A,** with words like <u>a</u>, <u>act</u> and <u>add</u>. The list ends with **Z** words, <u>zero</u> and <u>zoo</u>. The list is in alphabetical order from **A** to **Z**.
     After each word, there are sentences to tell you what the word means and how it is used. This is called the **definition** of the word. For example, you can read on this page a definition of **dig**: "To **dig** is to make a hole in the ground. Our dog likes to **dig** in the flower garden."

dictionary   A **dictionary** is a book that tells what words mean. **Dictionaries** also show how to spell words.

did   Have you finished your homework? Yes, I **did** all of it. **Did** is a form of the word DO. **Did** is used to tell about a thing that has already happened.

didn't   **Didn't** is a short way to say or write "did not." I got the book, but I **didn't** read it yet.

die   **Die** means to not live any more. That plant will **die** without water and sunlight.
—**dies, died, dying.**

diet   **1.** Your **diet** is the things you eat. Eating a lot of candy and sweet foods is not a good **diet.**
2. A **diet** is a way to lose weight. People who are on a **diet** don't eat a lot and don't eat certain foods.

different   Something that is **different** is not the same as another or others. I don't see Joe much this year because he goes to a **different** school now. Softball is a lot like baseball. The main **difference** is that softball uses a **different** ball.

difficult   Something that is **difficult** is hard to do. The test was very **difficult,** and no one in the class got a high mark.

dig   To **dig** is to make a hole in the ground. Our dog likes to **dig** in the flower garden.
—**digs, dug, digging.**

dinner   **Dinner** is the last meal of the day. People eat **dinner** at night or late in the afternoon. People sometimes call the last meal of the day **supper** if it is not a big meal.
A **dining room** is a room in a house for eating **dinner** and other meals.

dinosaur A **dinosaur** was an animal that lived millions of years ago. **Dinosaurs** were the biggest animals that ever lived on land.

This huge **dinosaur** was a brontosaurus.

direction   1. A **direction** is any way you look or go. We all looked in the **direction** the ball was hit to see where it went. 2. **Directions** are a list of rules for doing something. When we put my new bike together, we read the **directions** to see how to do it.

dirt **Dirt** is what the ground is made of. We dug up the **dirt** when we planted the flowers.

dirty Something that is **dirty** is not clean. Eddie had a **dirty** face and shirt from playing out in the mud.

discover When you **discover** something, you find it for the first time. Columbus **discovered** America in 1492.

discuss To **discuss** means to talk about something. Our teacher had us **discuss** the story we read. When you **discuss** something, that is called a **discussion.**

dish A **dish** is a thing to put food on when you eat. Most **dishes** are flat and round.

distance **Distance** means how far it is to a place. The **distance** from my home to my school is about one mile.

divide   1. To **divide** a thing is to make it into parts. There was only one orange left, so Matt and I **divided** it between us. 2. To **divide** a number is to find out how many times it has another number in it. 8 **divided** by 2 is 4. When you **divide** two numbers, it is called **division.**

do   1. **Do** means to make a thing happen. Josh has to **do** some work in the yard. I know you'll **do** a good job on your paper. 2. **Do** is used to ask questions. **Do** you want some more milk? —**does, did, doing.**

doctor   A **doctor** is a person who helps sick people get well.

does   **Does** is a form of the word DO. What time **does** the movie start?

doesn't   **Doesn't** is a short way to say or write "does not." A train **doesn't** go as fast as an airplane.

dog   A **dog** is an animal. Many people have **dogs** as pets.

doll   A **doll** is a toy to play with. **Dolls** may look like babies or like people of any age.

dollar   A **dollar** is an amount of money. One **dollar** is the same as 100 cents. The train ride costs two **dollars**.

don't   **Don't** is a short way to say or write "do not." **Don't** touch that paint. It's still wet.

done   **Done** is a form of DO. It tells about something that has already happened. When his project was all **done**, Willie put away all his papers and books.

door   A **door** opens or closes the way into a room or other place. Ellen left the front **door** open, and the dog got out.

dot   A **dot** is a tiny round mark. There is a **dot** at the top of the letter "i."

double   **Double** means there are two of something. A **double** play in baseball means you get two outs on one play.

down   To go **down** means to go from a higher place to a lower one. If you drop a ball on a hill, the ball will roll **down** the hill. As the day ends, the sun goes **down** in the sky.

dozen   A **dozen** is a group of 12 things. Mom bought a **dozen** eggs at the store.

drank   With lunch I **drank** two glasses of milk. **Drank** is a form of the word DRINK.

draw   When you **draw** you make a picture on paper. The thing you draw is a **drawing**. —**draws, drew, drawn, drawing**.

dream   When you sleep and have pictures in your mind, you are **dreaming**. In **dreams** there are silly or strange things that can't happen in real life. —**dreams, dreamed** or **dreamt, dreaming**.

dress 1. A **dress** is a thing that girls and women wear. **Dresses** have a top part and a **skirt.**
2. To **dress** means to put clothes on. He's old enough now to **dress** himself without any help.

drew Jean **drew** a picture of her cat. **Drew** is a form of DRAW.

drink When you **drink** water or juice, you take it into your body through your mouth.
—**drinks, drank, drunk, drinking.**

drive When you **drive** a car, you sit in it and make it go. Dad **drives** us to school every day. His job is **driving** a truck.
—**drives, drove, driven, driving.**

driver A person who drives something is a **driver**. The bus **driver** took our class to the park.

drop To **drop** something is to let it fall down. Lisa **dropped** her pencil on the ground.
—**drops, dropped, dropping.**

drove He **drove** the car to the store. **Drove** is a form of DRIVE.

drug 1. A **drug** is a thing you take to make you feel better when you are sick.
2. Some **drugs** are very bad for you if you take them too much.

dry When a thing is **dry**, it is not wet. It has no water in it or on it. Helen **dried** the dishes after dinner. A **dryer** is a thing to make clothes **dry**.
—**dries, dried, drying.**

duck A **duck** is a bird. **Ducks** like to live on or near water.

dug **Dug** is a form of DIG. The rabbit **dug** a hole in the ground.

during **During** is in the time that something is happening. Our power went off **during** the TV show and we missed it.

dust **Dust** is very tiny pieces of dirt. Something that is covered with **dust** is **dusty.**

dropping a letter from a word If you let something fall to the ground, you **drop** it. But **drop** can also mean that you take something off. If you write <u>isn't</u> instead of <u>is not</u>, you <u>drop</u> the letter **o** from <u>is not</u>.
   When you drop the **o** from <u>is not</u> to make <u>isn't</u>, a mark goes in place of the **o**. The mark looks like this **'** . This mark is called an **apostrophe**. We say **apostrophe** as "uh-pos-tru-fee." When you drop a letter to make a word like <u>isn't</u>, remember to write the apostrophe.

E e

a b c d e f g h i j k l m n o p q r s t u v w x y z

each **Each** means every one. **Each** child on the team will get to play in the game. The tickets sell for one dollar **each.**

eagle An **eagle** is a large bird with long wings. **Eagles** can fly very high above the ground.

ear You have an **ear** on each side of your head. You use your **ears** to hear things.

early **1.** When you are there before a thing happens, you are **early.** We're **early.** The movie doesn't start for half an hour. **2.** The first part of the day is the **early** part. Five o'clock is **early** in the morning.

earn When you get money for working, you **earn** it. Katie **earns** money taking care of her baby sister.

earth **1.** The **earth** is the place where all people live. The **earth** is called a **planet.** It has animals, plants, oceans, land, and air. **2. Earth** is also the ground or dirt. When the ground shakes, that is called an **earthquake.**

east **East** is a direction on the earth. The sun comes up in the **east.** New York is in the **eastern** part of the United States.

easy When you can do a thing with no trouble, it is **easy.** An **easy** thing is not hard to do. The spelling test was **easy** and I got all the words right.

eat You **eat** when you put food in your mouth and chew it so that it can go down to your stomach. I **eat** dinner at six o'clock every night. **—eats, ate, eating.**

edge   The end part of a thing is its **edge.** That glass is too near the **edge** of the table, and it might fall off.
—edges.

education   When you learn about things in school, you are getting an **education.**

egg   A baby bird comes out of an **egg** when it is born. People eat chicken **eggs** for breakfast.

eight   **Eight** is the word for the number **8.** It comes after seven and before nine.

either   **Either** means one thing or the other. With lunch, you can drink **either** milk or juice.

elbow   Your **elbow** is where your arm bends in the middle.

election   An **election** is when you pick a person by a vote. The President of the U. S. is chosen in an **election.** Lisa won the **election** for class president.

electricity   **Electricity** is a kind of power that makes lights go on. It makes things like radios and televisions work. It goes through wires. A thing that uses power from **electricity** is **electric.**

elementary school   A school that has kindergarten to sixth grade is an **elementary school.**

elephant   An **elephant** is a very large, gray animal. It has big ears, and a long nose called a **trunk. Elephants** are the biggest animals that live on land.

The **elephant** on the left is from India. The one on the right is from Africa.

elevator   An **elevator** carries people up or down in a building.

else   Another thing, other than what is there, is something **else.** I know Jo was at the party. Who **else** came? Don't touch that glass or **else** you'll cut your finger.

emergency   An **emergency** is when something bad happens that has to be taken care of right away. A fire in a big building is an **emergency.**

ending a word with -ed "I <u>walk</u> home from school every day. I <u>walked</u> home from school yesterday with my friend Suzie." Do you see the difference between these sentences? <u>Walk</u> tells about something that happens all the time. <u>Walked</u> tells about one thing that happened before now. <u>Walk</u> is a **verb**. <u>Walked</u> is the **past time** (or **past tense**) of this verb. To use the past time, you add **ed** to the end of the word. You can see an example on this page, <u>end**ed**</u>. If a word already has **e** at the end, drop this **e** before you add **ed,** as in <u>escap**ed**</u> (also on this page).

empty   When a thing is **empty,** there is nothing in it. The dog's water dish was **empty**. You can put your toys in that **empty** box.

end   The last part of a thing is the **end**. Our house is at the **end** of Oak Street. We scored a goal as the game **ended** and won 1-0. (See the box on this page.) —**ends, ended, ending.**

energy   **Energy** makes things move and work. You can't see it, but you can see how it makes things go. Oil and electricity have **energy**. The sun, fire, and running water have **energy,** too.

engine   An **engine** is a machine that makes things move. A car **engine** burns gas to make it go. This plane has three jet **engines**.

enough   **Enough** means you have as much as you need. Jill has **enough** money to buy her mother a birthday present.

enter   If you **enter** a room, you go into it. The way to go inside a building is called its **entrance.**

equal   If two numbers are **equal,** they are the same amount. One dollar is **equal** to 100 cents.

escape   **Escape** means to get away or run away. The mice **escaped** from the box and ran all around the classroom.

especially   **Especially** means very much. Kim was **especially** tired after running a mile. I like ice cream, **especially** chocolate.

even   **1. Even** means more than some other. Brian is **even** taller than his dad is.
2. A thing is **even** when it is straight. I made the bed so that the covers were neat and **even.**
3. When both sides are the same, they are **even. Even numbers** like 2, 4, 6, 8, and 10 can be divided right in half.

evening **Evening** is the time of day when it starts to get dark. It is between afternoon and night.

ever **Ever** means at all times or at any time. Have you **ever** been to Disney World?

every **Every** means each one. She loves that TV show and watches it **every** day. **Every** house on the street had a mail box in front of it.

everyone **Everyone** means every person. **Everyone** in my family has brown hair. **Everybody** means the same thing as everyone. **Everybody** in our class came to the party.

everything **Everything** means all things. A big wave came up on the beach and **everything** on our blanket got wet.

exact When something is just right, it is **exact.** Our town has about 15,000 people. The **exact** number is 14,872.

exactly **Exactly** means in an exact way. The train will leave at **exactly** 8:00.

example An **example** is one of a certain kind of things. Many large wild animals live in Africa, for **example,** the lion.

excellent Something **excellent** is very, very good. The teacher said that Natalie did an **excellent** history report, and he gave her an A+.

except **Except** means all but one thing. All the boys **except** Tony had pizza. He had a hot dog. All the months have 30 or 31 days, **except** February.

excited If you are **excited,** you feel very happy and lively. The girls were **excited** when their team won the soccer game.

exciting When a thing is full of fun and surprises, it is **exciting.** Ellen's birthday was a very **exciting** day for her.

exclamation marks "Stop**!**" "Please help me**!**" "Get out of the way**!**" Notice that an **exclamation mark** (**!**) tells you that something special or important is being said. You would not write, "She bought a hat!" There is nothing special or different about this sentence. It does not need an exclamation mark. It should have a period (**.**) instead. But you could write, "I won't wear that hat**!**" This would show that the person is upset and is speaking loudly. That is what an **exclamation** is.

excuse   An **excuse** is the reason why you didn't do something. Students must bring an **excuse** to the office telling why they stayed home from school. Billy finished eating and asked if he could be **excused** from the table.
—**excuses, excused, excusing.**

exercise   When you move your body in a special way, you **exercise. Exercises** make you feel good and make your body stronger. Running, swimming, and playing a sport or game are all kinds of **exercise.**

exit   An **exit** is the way you can leave a place. In case of a fire in the building, walk quickly and carefully to the nearest **exit.** We get off the main road just ahead, at the Johnson Street **exit.**

expect   **Expect** means to look or wait for something to happen. We **expect** Grandpa to visit us this week. The Riley family is **expecting** their new baby to be born soon.
—**expects, expected, expecting.**

expensive   A thing that costs a lot of money is **expensive.** She didn't buy the dress. It was too **expensive.** The movie star lived in a big, **expensive** house.

experience   When you do something or something happens to you, that is an **experience.** Mrs. Warren has been teaching for a long time. She has a lot of **experience** as a teacher.

explain   To **explain** something means to tell about it so that someone knows it. Our teacher **explains** our work to us. Mom **explained** why she didn't want us to play in the woods. When you explain something, it is called an **explanation.**

explore   When you look around in a new place, you **explore** it. A person who does this is an **explorer.** Two men named Lewis and Clark **explored** the western United States in the early days of our country.

extra   When there is one more than you need, it is **extra.** We had an **extra** ticket to the play, so we gave it to Eddie. I always carry **extra** money in case I need to call home.

eye   An **eye** is part of your body. You have two **eyes** on your face. You use your **eyes** to see things. The hair above the **eyes** is called the **eyebrows.**

F f

a b c d e f g h i j k l m n o p q r s t u v w x y z

face Your **face** is the front part of your head. Your eyes, nose, and mouth are parts of your **face.** If you **face** something, you are turned toward it.

fact A **fact** is something that is true. It is a **fact** that the earth moves around the sun. That book has a lot of interesting **facts** about American history.

fair 1. When a thing is **fair,** it is done in the right way. The race was not **fair** because one of the runners started to run too soon. **2.** A **fair** is a place where people get together to show things or to have fun. Many **fairs** have food to buy and games to play.

fall 1. Fall means to come down from a high place. Rain was **falling** all day. She will **fall** off the horse if she doesn't hold on.

2. Fall is a time of year. It comes after summer and before winter. In many places, leaves change colors and **fall** off the trees then. **—falls, fell, fallen, falling.**

false Something that is **false** is not true or real. It is **false** to say that the world is flat.

family A **family** is a mother and father and their children. Grandparents, aunts, and uncles are also part of a **family.**

famous A person who is **famous** is known by lots of people. George Washington is a **famous** American. Many TV and movie stars are **famous.**

far If a thing is **far,** it is a long way away. Japan and China are **far** from the United States. How **far** is your house from school?

farm   A **farm** is a large piece of land. On a **farm,** plants and animals are raised for food. A **farmer** is a person who lives and works on a **farm.**

A large **farm** in Alberta, Canada.

farther   **Farther** means a longer distance. I have to walk **farther** than my friend Dan does to get to school. I live **farther** away from school than he does.

fast   Something that is **fast** moves very quickly. Josh wins a lot of races at school because he is a very **fast** runner. A plane can go **faster** than a car.

fat   **Fat** means heavy and big around. Pigs are **fat** animals.

father   A **father** is a man who has a child or children. Dad and Daddy are names that children call their **father.**

fault   If something bad happens because of you, it is your **fault.** It was my **fault** that the dog got out. I left the door wide open.

favor   A **favor** is something nice or kind that you do to help another person. Do me a **favor** and help me wash the dishes.

favorite   If something is your **favorite,** it is the thing you like the most. Her **favorite** dinner is chicken with rice and corn.

feather   A **feather** is a light, soft thing that covers a bird's skin. A bird's **feathers** help it to fly.

feed   To **feed** means to give food to. Mom has to **feed** my baby brother because he is too little to **feed** himself yet. I **fed** my dog a big dinner after our long walk. **—feeds, fed, feeding.**

feel   **1.** To **feel** something means to touch it or know it is touching you. When I opened the door, I could **feel** the cold wind against my face.
2. To **feel** means to be a certain way. Brett **felt** bad about losing his new jacket.

feet   **Feet** means "more than one foot." My dad is six **feet** tall.

fiction Made-up stories are called **fiction.** Fiction tells about make-believe people or animals. The things that happen in fiction are not real. Stories about the real world are called **nonfiction.**

Here's an example of the difference. The author E. B. White wrote "Charlotte's Web." This is **fiction.** It's about a farm where the animals talk to each other and a spider knows how to write. E. B. White also wrote "Farewell, My Lovely." This is **nonfiction.** It is a true story about a car that Mr. White had owned when he was a young man.

fell Christine **fell** off her bicycle and cut her knee. **Fell** is a form of the word FALL.

felt I **felt** sick yesterday, so I stayed in bed. **Felt** is a form of the word FEEL.

female A **female** is a girl or a woman. A **female** chicken is called a hen.

fence A **fence** is like a wall. It is put up to keep things in or out of a certain place. **Fences** are made of things like wood or wire.

few A **few** is a small number, not too many. She almost never gets sick. She has missed only a **few** days of school this year.

field A **field** is a large, flat area with no trees. Farmers grow plants or keep animals in a **field.** Sports such as baseball and soccer are played on **fields.**

fight A **fight** can happen when people are very mad at each other. When people **fight,** they may yell or try to hurt each other. Two countries may **fight** against each other in a war. —**fights, fought, fighting.**

fill To **fill** a thing means to put as much into it as it will hold. **Fill** this cup with milk all the way up to the top. The room was **filled** with people.

film **Film** is the special paper you put in a camera to take a picture. A **film** is also another name for a MOVIE.

find 1. To **find** a thing means to get it after it was lost. I **found** the library book under my bed. 2. To **find** also means to come upon something that was not known before. Did you **find** the answer to that math problem? —**finds, found, finding.**

finish "I have to do a science project for school. The teacher says we have to <u>finish</u> it by March 1st. We have to <u>complete</u> all our work by then." In these sentences, the words <u>finish</u> and <u>complete</u> have the same meaning. They both mean "bring to an end." If a word means the same thing as another word, then it is a **synonym** for that other word. In this book, we often use a synonym to explain what a word means. For example, we say "<u>Correct</u> means right." <u>Correct</u> and <u>right</u> are synonyms. If you know what <u>right</u> means, then you'll know what <u>correct</u> means.

fine **Fine** means very good. How are you today? I'm just **fine,** thank you. Carlos did a **fine** job on his science project.

finger A **finger** is one of the long parts at the end of your hand. We have five **fingers** on each hand.

finish To **finish** is to get to the end of something. I can watch TV after I **finish** my homework. The place where a race ends is called the **finish** line. (See the box on this page.)

fire A **fire** is the flame from something that is burning. **Fires** are hot and give off light. A **firefighter** is a person whose job is to put out fires. A **fireplace** is a special place to hold a fire.

first A thing that is **first** comes before everything else. The **first** letter of the alphabet is 'A.' The **first** month is January.

fish A **fish** is an animal that lives under water. Many kinds of **fish** are good to eat. **Fishing** means trying to catch a **fish.**

fit Something that **fits** is the right size. It is not too big or too little. These shoes are too small. They don't **fit** me any more.

five **Five** is the word for the number **5.** It comes after four and before six.

fix **1.** To **fix** something means to make it work right. Our TV set has no sound. We have to get it **fixed.**
2. Fix also means to do a certain thing. When Mom isn't home, I can **fix** my own lunch.
—**fixes, fixed, fixing.**

flag A **flag** is a piece of cloth with special colors and designs on it. The **flag** of the United States is red, white, and blue and has stars and stripes.

flame A **flame** is the light color that you see moving up and down in a fire.

flash A thing that **flashes** makes a fast light for a short time. Lightning **flashes** in the sky.

flashlight A **flashlight** is a small light that you can carry in your hand and turn on and off.

flat Something that is **flat** has a smooth, even surface. **Flat** land has no mountains or hills.

flavor The **flavor** of food is how it tastes. Fresh orange juice has a sweet **flavor.** That store sells many **flavors** of ice cream.

flew The bird **flew** away when it saw me. **Flew** is a form of the word FLY.

floor 1. The **floor** is the bottom part of a room. You stand and walk on the floor.
2. A **floor** is a part of a building. My room is upstairs, on the second **floor** of our house.

flower A **flower** is a pretty part on a plant. **Flowers** come in many colors and shapes. Some **flowers** smell pretty. Daisies and roses are **flowers.**

fly 1. To **fly** means to use wings to move through the air. Birds fly south in the winter. When I went to Florida it was the first time I'd ever **flown** in a plane. 2. A **fly** is a kind of insect that moves through the air.
—**flies, flew, flown, flying.**

fog **Fog** is like a cloud that sits on the ground. When there is **fog,** the air looks gray and you can't see very far. **Fog** is made of tiny drops of water.

Fog lies over the hills of California.

fold If you **fold** a thing, you put one part of it over another part. Mom **folded** up the clean wash before she put it away.

follow To **follow** means to come after something. The letter 'B' **follows** the letter 'A' in the alphabet. My dog **followed** me to the store.

45

food **Food** is what we eat. All people, animals, and plants need **food** to stay alive. Bread, cheese, meat, corn, and oranges are different kinds of **food.**

foot **1.** Your **foot** is a part of your body at the end of your leg. You stand and walk on your **feet.** **2. Foot** is also a word used to tell how long or how tall a thing is. There are 12 inches in a **foot.**

football **Football** is a game played by two teams. The ball for this game is also called a **football.** The team with the ball tries to get it down the field, and the other team tries to stop them.

for I got a present **for** Dan. It was **for** his birthday. His party lasted **for** an hour. Then it was time to leave **for** home.

foreign A country that is not the one you live in is a **foreign** country. To an American, Canada is a **foreign** country.

forest A **forest** is a big place with many trees.

forever Something that goes on **forever** will never end. That big tree is so old, it looks like it's been there **forever.**

forget If you **forget** a thing, you don't remember it. Joe **forgot** his lunch and had to buy lunch at school. It's cold outside, so don't **forget** to wear a jacket.

fork A **fork** is a thing you eat with. It has a handle and long, pointed parts on one end.

form **1.** The **form** of a thing is what it looks like. A ring has the **form** of a circle. **2. Form** also means one kind of thing. "Biggest" is a **form** of the word "big." (See the box on this page.) **3.** A **form** is a paper you have to write things on. Meg wrote her name and address on a **form** when she got a library card.

---

forms of a word If you look under the letter **W** in this dictionary, you will find the word <u>work</u>. You might use this word to say, "I <u>work</u> hard in school." But you could also use this word <u>work</u> in other ways. "Dad <u>work</u>ed late at his office last night." "My Mom <u>work</u>s in our school library." "I've been <u>work</u>ing on a report for school." "My sister is a hard <u>work</u>er." These are all **forms** of the word <u>work</u>. The word <u>work</u> itself is called the **base** or **root form.** The idea is that the other forms grow out from the root form <u>work</u>, the way a plant grows from its roots.

forward   **Forward** means to the front. The teacher told us to come **forward** to the front of the room as she called our names.

fought   The U. S. **fought** in World War Two. **Fought** is a form of the word FIGHT.

found   I **found** a quarter on the way home from school. **Found** is a form of the word FIND.

four   **Four** is the word for the number **4.** It comes after three and before five.

fox   A **fox** is an animal that looks like a dog. It has red fur, a long tail, and a pointed nose.

The red **fox** lives in North America.

free   **1.** Something that is **free** doesn't cost any money. You have to pay to park here in the daytime, but at night it's **free.**

2. Free also means that you are not held and can do what you want. In a **free** country, people can say what they want. They don't keep their dog tied up. He just runs **free** all over town.

freeze   When a thing **freezes,** it gets very, very cold. If water **freezes,** it becomes hard and turns into ice. A **freezer** is a thing that keeps food very cold. **—freezes, froze, frozen, freezing.**

fresh   **1.** Something that is **fresh** is new. They had **fresh** corn from their garden for dinner. **2. Fresh** also means clean and clear. It felt good to be out in the **fresh** air. **Fresh water** in a lake or river does not have salt in it the way ocean water does.

Friday   **Friday** is a day of the week. It comes after Thursday and before Saturday.

friend   A **friend** is a person that you like and who likes you. Tod always wants to sit next to his **friend** Billy on the school bus.

friendly   A **friendly** person is nice to people. Jan is a **friendly** girl who always has a smile and a nice word for everyone.

frog   A **frog** is an animal. It lives both in water and on land.

The American **bullfrog** is a kind of **frog.**

from   Jamie got a letter **from** her cousin. This cheese comes **from** France. The park is about a mile **from** here. One **from** four leaves three. Bread is made **from** flour.

front   The **front** is the part that is away from the back. People were standing in **front** of the store, waiting for it to open. The name of a book is shown on its **front** cover.

froze   The lake **froze** last night, and it's all covered with ice now. **Froze** and **frozen** are forms of the word FREEZE.

fruit   **Fruit** is a kind of sweet food that grows on plants. There are many kinds of **fruit.** Apples, oranges, and cherries are **fruit.**

full   Something that is **full** can't hold any more. The bus was **full.** All the seats were taken and no one else could get on. I felt really **full** after eating such a big dinner.

fun   If you are having **fun,** you are having a good time. I really have **fun** when I go to the beach with my friends.

funny   1. Something that makes you laugh is **funny.** Anna told a **funny** joke about an elephant in a bathtub.
2. **Funny** can also mean strange or not right. The house was dark. Beth thought that was **funny,** because she had left a light on when she went out.

fur   **Fur** is the hair that covers an animal. Cats have soft **fur.** The **fur** of some animals is used to make **fur** coats.

furniture   **Furniture** is the name for tables, chairs, beds, desks, and other things like that. **Furniture** can be moved around.

future   The **future** is any time after right now. The **future** has not happened yet. I did it wrong that time, but in the **future** I won't make the same mistake.

G g

gain   If you **gain** something, it means you add it to what you have. Children **gain** weight as they get older.

game   A **game** is something you do for fun or to win. Many **games** are played with a ball, such as baseball. Other **games** are played with cards or on a board or a computer.

garage   A **garage** is a place to keep a car. A place where cars are fixed or taken care of is also called a **garage.**

garbage   **Garbage** is food that is not wanted. **Garbage** is thrown away in garbage cans or bags.

garden   A **garden** is a piece of land near a house for growing plants. Flowers, fruits, and vegetables grow in **gardens.**

gas   **Gas** is a liquid that is used to make machines work. A car engine burns **gas** to make it go. **Gas** is a short word for **gasoline.**

gate   A **gate** is a door in a place. There are **gates** in fences.

gave   Stacy **gave** her friend Lisa a book for her birthday. **Gave** is a form of the word GIVE.

get   **1.** When you take a thing and have it, you **get** it. I **get** a birthday present from my Grandma every year. Laura **gets** good marks in school.
2. When you go to a place, you **get** there. Can you **get** to the city on this road?
3. Get can also mean that you feel a certain way. We can say that someone **got** sick, **got** tired, or **got** hungry.
—**gets, got, gotten, getting.**

49

ghost A **ghost** is a make-believe thing in a story. **Ghosts** are dead people who come back to scare living people.

giant A **giant** is a very, very big person or thing. Long ago, **giant** animals called dinosaurs lived on the earth.

gift A **gift** is something nice that a person gives. Many people give each other **gifts** at Christmas.

giraffe A **giraffe** is a very, very tall animal. **Giraffes** have very long necks and long legs.

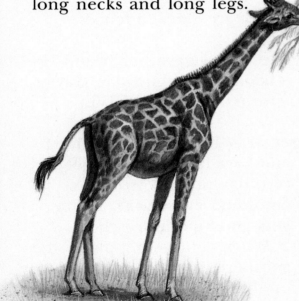

The **giraffe** lives in flat areas in Africa.

girl A **girl** is a female child. **Girls** will grow up to be women. Jane is the tallest **girl** in our class.

give When you let someone have something, you **give** it to them. My parents **give** money to help the poor people in our town. Scott has **given** his old toys to his younger brother.
—**gives, gave, given, giving.**

glad When you feel **glad,** you are happy. Greg was **glad** to be invited to the party.

glass 1. **Glass** is a thing you can see through. **Glass** is hard but it is easy to break. When it breaks, it is very sharp. Windows are made of **glass.**
2. A **glass** is something to put a drink in. **Glasses** are tall, round, and made of glass or plastic.
3. People wear **glasses** to help them see better. These are also called **eyeglasses. Sunglasses** are used to protect the eyes from bright sunlight.

glove You wear a **glove** on your hand. **Gloves** fit over each finger. People wear **gloves** in the winter to keep their hands warm and dry.

glue **Glue** is something that is used to stick things together. **Glue** is thick and wet but it is hard when it dries. Dad **glued** the broken plate together again.

50

go   The word **go** is a verb, like <u>walk</u>, <u>kick</u>, <u>jump</u>, <u>miss</u>, or <u>stay</u>. But <u>go</u> is not the same as those words. To tell about what happened before, you add **ed** to those words. "I was sick today. I <u>stay</u>**ed** home from school." But you can't say, "We <u>goed</u> to the movies" or "I have <u>goed</u> to this school since first grade." You have to say, "We <u>went</u> to the movies" and "I have <u>gone</u> to this school since first grade." We say that <u>stay</u> is a **regular verb**, because it forms the past time in the usual way. <u>Go</u> is an **irregular verb** (not regular). It forms the past time in a different way.

go   To **go** means to move from one place to another. Let's **go** to see Grandma today. Children have to **go** to school. Where has my little dog **gone?**
—**goes, went, gone, going.**

goal   A **goal** is a thing you try to reach or get. In soccer you try to kick the ball into a **goal.**

going   Be careful when you're **going** down those steps. It's dark out. I think it's **going to** rain. **Going** is a form of the word GO. We use **going to** to tell about something that will happen.

gold   **Gold** is a kind of metal. **Gold** is soft and yellow. It is worth a lot of money. **Gold** is also the name for a bright yellow color.

gone   My book is **gone.** I can't find it anywhere. The baby is quiet. I guess he's **gone** to sleep. **Gone** is a form of the word GO.

good   Something that is **good** is not bad. It is the way you want it to be. The sun was out and it was warm. It was a **good** day to play outside. The teacher said my paper was very **good.** She read it to the whole class.

good-bye   When you go away or someone else goes away, you say **good-bye.** You also say **good-bye** after you talk on the telephone. **Good-bye** is also spelled **good-by.**

goose   A **goose** is a bird that is like a duck. Most **geese** live on or near water.

gorilla   A **gorilla** is a large animal. **Gorillas** are apes, and look something like a monkey.

got   Wendy **got** a new watch after she lost her old one. Tracy has **gotten** a lot taller since the last time I saw her. **Got** and **gotten** are forms of GET.

government A **government** is the people and the rules that help run a country, state, or city. The President is the highest officer in the United States **government**.

grab To **grab** a thing is to take hold of it in a quick, rough way. I **grabbed** the dog by the neck as he tried to run out the door.

grade 1. A **grade** is a year of work in a school. Paul is now in the sixth **grade.**
2. A **grade** tells how well work was done in school. She got a grade of 'A' on her math test.

grain A **grain** is a seed. Plants such as wheat, corn, and rice have **grains.**

grain These foods are made from **grains** of wheat.

grandparent A **grandparent** is a grandmother or grandfather. Your **grandfather** is the father of your mother or father. Your **grandmother** is the mother of your mother or father.

grape A **grape** is a kind of fruit. A **grape** is small and round. **Grapes** grow together on a **vine.**

grapefruit A **grapefruit** is a kind of fruit. **Grapefruits** are yellow and have a sour taste.

grass Grass is a kind of plant. People grow **grass** in their yards. This grass is called a **lawn.** Wheat, corn, and rice are **grasses** that are used for food.

gray Gray is a color that is between black and white. When it rains, the sky looks **gray.**

great 1. Great means very, very good. The author William Shakespeare wrote **great** plays. I had a **great** time at the party.
2. Great means very big or very important. The **Great Lakes** are the biggest lakes in the U. S.

green Green is a color. Grass is **green.** The leaves on a tree are **green** in summer.

grew   We **grew** corn in our garden last summer. **Grew** is a form of the word GROW.

ground   The **ground** is the dirt and rock outside. Flowers and plants grow in the **ground.** The **ground** had turned to mud after the heavy rain.

group   A **group** is many things that are together. Lions live together in a **group** of 20 or 30 animals. Our class has three reading **groups.**

grow   To **grow** is to get bigger. A baby **grows** a lot in its first three years. When Lisa **grows** up, she wants to be a teacher. That tree has really **grown** since we planted it last year. —**grows, grew, grown, growing.**

grown-up   A **grown-up** is a person who is finished growing. Parents and other adults are **grown-ups.** (See the box on this page.)

guard   To **guard** a thing means to watch over it so that nothing bad happens. There are **guards** at a bank to make sure no one steals the money. —**guards, guarded, guarding.**

guess   You **guess** when you don't know the answer but are trying to find it. Mrs. Dale had us **guess** how many pennies there were in the big bottle on her desk. I'm not sure where Jeff is. I **guess** he went home.

guest   A **guest** is a person who comes to your house to visit. People who stay in a hotel are also called **guests.**

gun   A **gun** is a thing that shoots. **Guns** fire hard pieces of metal called **bullets.** Soldiers and police use **guns.**

gym   A **gym** is a large building for playing sports and doing exercises. Many schools have a **gym** as part of the school. **Gym** is a short word for **gymnasium.**

grown-up   Look above, at the word **grown-up**. Do you see something different about the word? There is a small line in the middle of the word, like this. **-** This line is called a **hyphen.** (Say it as "HIGH-fin.") We use a hyphen to join two words together as one. Grown is a word by itself, and so is up. A hyphen is also used in books and newspapers to break up a word that is too long to fit at the end of a line. Here's an **ex-ample.** One part of example is on one line, and one part is on the next.

H h

a b c d e f g **h** i j k l m n o p q r s t u v w x y z

had   I **had** my book when I came in, but now I can't find it. **Had** is a form of the word HAVE.

hair   **Hair** grows on the skin of people or animals. The **hair** on your head can grow very long.

half   If you cut something in **half,** you have two parts that are the same size. I don't want a whole glass of milk. Just give me **half** a glass.

hall   A **hall** is a part of a building that you walk through to get from one room to another. Our classroom is just down the **hall** from the library.

Halloween   **Halloween** is a day when children get dressed up in strange or funny ways. It is on October 31. Bobby dressed up as a clown for **Halloween.**

hamburger   A **hamburger** is a kind of food. It is made from meat that has been cut up.

hand   Your **hand** is part of your body. Your **hands** are on the ends of your arms.

handle   A **handle** is the part of a thing that your hand holds on to. A knife has a **handle** that you hold when you use it.

handsome   A man or boy is **handsome** when he looks good. Grandma told Tommy he looked very **handsome** with his new haircut.

hang   When you **hang** on to something, you hold on to it from below. The little boy was **hanging** on to his mother's hand and would not let go.
—**hangs, hung, hanging.**

54

have   The verb **have** is one of the most important words in English. It's a word that we use all the time. If you <u>have</u> something, it is yours. "Do you <u>have</u> any pets at home? Yes, I <u>have</u> a dog." The past form of **have** is **had**. "We <u>had</u> a cat, but it ran away."

If you <u>have to</u> do something, you must do it. "Children <u>have to</u> <u>go</u> to school." <u>Have</u> is also used with other verbs. "Lisa <u>has been</u> <u>working</u> on a paper for school for an hour. She <u>has not finished</u> it yet." Notice that you use the word **has** (a form of **have**) with <u>she</u> or <u>he</u> or <u>it</u>.

happen   If a thing is **happening,** it is going on right now. A big tree in our yard fell down. It **happened** during the storm last night. What **happened** to the car? It has a big scratch on the front door.

happy   When you feel **happy,** you are not sad. You feel very good. Judy felt **happy** when she got all 'A's on her report card.

hard   1. **Hard** means not soft. The walls and floor of a house are **hard.**
2. **Hard** also means not easy to do. My brother's high-school science book was **hard** for me to read.

has   My sister Karen **has** a new bike. A giraffe **has** a long neck. **Has** is a form of the word **have.**

hat   A **hat** is a thing you wear on your head. People wear **hats** to keep their heads warm.

hate   When you **hate** something you don't like it at all. Dad **hates** fish and never wants to eat it. I **hate** the color of that dress and I would never buy it.

have   1. When you **have** a thing, it is yours and it is with you. I **have** one brother and two sisters. They all **have** brown hair.
2. **Have** means that a certain thing is happening to you. You can **have** lunch, **have** a cold, or **have** fun. They **have** lived in that house since 1970.
3. **Have to** means that you must do something. Dad said I could go out to play, but I **have to** be home by six. (See the box on this page.)
—**has, had, having.**

he   Mark called for you before. **He** said **he** will call back later.

head   Your **head** is a part of your body. Your eyes, ears, nose, and mouth are parts of your **head.**

healthy If you are **healthy,** you are not sick. Eating the right foods is important to **health.**

hear To **hear** means to know about something by using your ears. I called out Jim's name, but he didn't **hear** me and just kept walking. She **heard** a noise and looked out to see what it was. —**hears, heard, hearing.**

heart 1. Your **heart** is a part of your body. It moves your blood to every part of your body. 2. A **heart** is also a shape. **Hearts** are used on cards to mean love.

heat **Heat** is something that makes things feel warm or hot. The **heat** from the fire warmed their faces. A car has a **heater** to keep the people inside warm on cold days. —**heats, heated, heating.**

heavy When a thing is **heavy,** it weighs a lot. A big rock or a box full of books is **heavy.**

height The **height** of a thing is how high it is. Ann's **height** is five feet two inches.

held I **held** the door open so that Mom could walk in. **Held** is a form of the word **hold.**

helicopter A **helicopter** is a machine that can fly. It has moving parts on top that turn around fast to keep it in the air.

A **helicopter** can fly straight up or down.

hello When people meet, they say **hello** to each other. People also say **hello** when they answer the telephone.

help When you **help** a person, you do something good for him or her. Ted's older sister **helped** him do his math homework.

her That girl goes to our school, but I don't know **her** name. It looked like my book, but Katie said it was **hers.** I wanted to help Mom, but she did it all **herself.**

here When a thing is **here,** it is in this place. Last week I went to play at Jason's house. Today he's coming over **here.**

hide   To **hide** a thing means to put it away in a place where it can't be seen. Children play a game where some **hide** and the others try to find them. Mom **hid** the cookies so that Chris wouldn't eat any before dinner. —**hides, hid, hidden, hiding.**

high   A thing that is **high** is far off the ground. I looked up and saw a plane **high** in the sky.

highway   A **highway** is a large main road. **Highways** do not have a lot of side streets going across them.

hill   A **hill** is a high piece of land. **Hills** are higher than flat land but not as high as mountains.

him   Dave asked us to give **him** a ride home. Mark fixed **himself** some soup for lunch.

his   Bob says that is **his** soccer ball. It must be **his,** because I have mine right here.

history   **History** is all the important things that have happened before now. If you study American **history** in school, you will learn about President Abraham Lincoln.

hit   To **hit** a thing means to touch it hard and fast. In baseball, you try to **hit** the ball. Jerry **hit** the table with his hand to show how mad he was. —**hits, hit, hitting.**

hold   When you **hold** a thing, you keep it in one place. Billy **held** the cat in his hands. Mom told me to **hold** still while she cut my hair. —**holds, held, holding.**

hole   A **hole** is an open space. They made a big **hole** in the ground to plant the tree.

holiday   A **holiday** is a special day. On many **holidays** the schools are closed and most people don't go to work.

hom- words   "The sun is hot here." "I hear the Smiths have a new baby son." Sun and son have the same sound, but they don't have the same meaning. The same thing is true for here and hear. Words like this are called **homophones.** Homo means "the same," and phone means "sound." You know another "sound" word like this, telephone. Some words not only have the same sound, but even the same spelling. An example is the bat that flies around and the bat you use to hit a ball. These words are **homographs.** Homograph means "the same writing."

home   The place where you live is your **home.**

homework   **Homework** is the work you do at home for school.

honest   To be **honest** is to tell the truth and try to do what is right.

hope   When we **hope** for a thing we want it to come true. I **hope** Mary can come to my party.

horse   A **horse** is a large animal that people can ride on. **Horses** have a long neck and tail.

hospital   A **hospital** is a large building where sick or hurt people stay. Nurses and doctors work at **hospitals.**

hot   When a thing is **hot,** it is not cold. In the summer, we have a lot of **hot** days here. If a thing is very **hot,** it can burn you.

hot dog   A **hot dog** is a long, thin food. It is made of meat.

hotel   A **hotel** is a building with rooms where people stay when they are away from home.

hour   An **hour** is an amount of time. There are 60 minutes in one **hour** and 24 **hours** in a day.

house   A **house** is a building where a family lives.

how   **How** much does that dress cost? Mom showed me **how** to use her computer.

huge   Something **huge** is very, very big. The whale is a **huge** animal.

human   A **human** is a man, woman, or child. People are called **human** beings.

hundred   **Hundred** is the word for the number **100.**

hungry   When you are **hungry,** you want to eat.

hunt   When you **hunt** for a thing, you look for it. A **hunter hunts** for wild animals.

hurry   When you **hurry,** you do things fast. Ben got up late and had to **hurry** to catch his bus.

hurt   If something is **hurt** it feels bad. Penny **hurt** her leg when she fell. Ted was **hurt** when his friend laughed at his mistake.

husband   A **husband** is a married man. **Husbands** and wives are married to each other.

I i   J j

a b c d e f g h **i j** k l m n o p q r s t u v w x y z

I **I** is the word you use to talk about yourself.

ice **Ice** is water that has become hard and solid. Water turns to **ice** when the air gets very cold.

ice cream **Ice cream** is a frozen dessert that tastes sweet. It comes in many different flavors.

idea An **idea** is something you think of in your mind. **Ideas** can be about many different things. Cathy had a good **idea** for a story she wanted to write.

if **If** it's a nice day tomorrow, we can go swimming. Jack doesn't know yet **if** he can go to the game with us.

ill **Ill** means to be sick. Tom stayed home from school because he was **ill.**

I'll **I'll** is a short way to say or write "I will." Someone's at the door. **I'll** see who it is.

I'm **I'm** is a short way to say or write "I am." **I'm** sorry I can't go with you today.

imagine To **imagine** something is to have a picture of it in your mind. The little girl **imagined** what it would be like if she were a famous movie star.

important When something is **important,** it means a lot. It's **important** to eat the right food and get enough sleep at night.

in Mary held the baby **in** her arms. We live **in** a big city.

inch An **inch** is a way to tell how long things are. Twelve **inches** is the same as one **foot.**

information   **Information** is a set of facts about something. That book will give you lots of **information** about wild animals.

insect   An **insect** is a very small animal with wings and six legs. Bees and ants are **insects.**

inside   The **inside** is what is not outside. There was a light over the front door, but the **inside** of the house was dark. The fruit of an orange is **inside** a hard skin.

instead   **Instead** means in place of something else. There was no milk left, so I had some juice **instead**. He wanted to watch TV **instead** of doing his homework.

interest   When you have an **interest** in something, you like to do it or want to know about it. Sarah is **interested** in animals. There was an **interesting** story about the City Zoo in the newspaper today.

into   It started to rain hard, so we all went **into** the house. The man cut the pizza **into** six pieces.

invent   **Invent** means to make something that no one has ever made before. Thomas Edison **invented** the electric light. A thing that is made in this way is an **invention**.

invite   When you **invite** people, you ask them to do something with you. Kelly **invited** her friend Anne to stay over at her house for the night. An **invitation** is a note or card that asks you to come to something.

iron   **Iron** is a very hard thing that comes from the earth. **Iron** is used to make cars, machines, and many other things.

is   It **is** a nice day today. The sky **is** blue. Tom **is** coming to see us. **Is** is a form of the word BE. You use **is** with "he," "she," or "it."

I or me?   You can use either **I** or **me** to tell about yourself. But the two words are used in different ways. **I** is used in the **subject** (or naming part) of a sentence. **Me** is used in the **predicate** (or telling part) of a sentence.

"Me went to the park with my sister." You know that's wrong, don't you? It should be "**I** went." But what about this? "My sister and me went to the park." This too is wrong. **Me** cannot be the subject of a sentence. "My sister and **I**" is correct. You can see this if you take away the other part of the subject. "My sister and me went to the park." You can tell that "Me went to the park" is wrong.

island An **island** is a piece of land that has water all around it. There are many **islands** in the Pacific Ocean. The state of Hawaii is made up of **islands.**

This **island** is in San Francisco Bay.

isn't **Isn't** is a short way to say or write "is not." This **isn't** my book. It must be yours. Wade **isn't** in school today. He must be sick.

it **It** is what we call an animal or a thing. Mary watched the car as **it** drove away. Is **it** time for dinner already? When John goes to school, he leaves his dog home by **itself.**

its A tiger has stripes on **its** body. **Its** fur is orange and black.

it's **It's** is a short way to say or write "it is." The Browns just bought a new car. **It's** blue with a white top.

jacket A **jacket** is a light coat. You wear a jacket when it is cool outside.

jar A **jar** is a heavy glass or bottle. A **jar** usually has a wide opening on top and no handles.

jealous If you are **jealous,** you wish you had something that someone else has. Matt was **jealous** of his friend's new bike and wished that he had one too.

jet A **jet** is a kind of airplane. It has engines that move it by burning gas and pushing it very fast out a small hole. These engines are also called **jets.**

jewel A **jewel** is a special kind of stone. **Jewels** are very pretty. They are usually expensive. Diamonds are a kind of **jewel.**

jewelry **Jewelry** is something pretty that you wear. Rings are **jewelry. Jewelry** can be made of gold, silver, or another metal.

job 1. A **job** is the work that a person does. My mother has a **job** as a nurse at the hospital. 2. A **job** is any work that has to be done. Picking up all the dead leaves and grass in the yard was a big **job.**

join   1. To **join** things is to put them together. The class **joined** hands to make a circle. Two large rivers **join** near the city of St. Louis, Missouri.
2. Join also means to become a part of a group. Ben **joined** the school soccer team and will play his first game next week.

joke   A **joke** is something you say or do to make people laugh. Erica told a funny **joke** about a dog that could talk. We played a **joke** on Steve and pretended we didn't know who he was.

joy   **Joy** is a feeling of being very happy. The whole family was filled with **joy** when their new baby was born.

judge   A **judge** is a person who decides things about the law. A **judge** is in charge of a **court** where cases of law are taken care of. When you **judge** something, you decide what it is like or what to do about it.

juice   **Juice** is a drink. **Juice** is made by taking the liquid out of foods such as oranges, apples, or tomatoes. A food with a lot of liquid in it is **juicy**. Oranges are a **juicy** kind of fruit.

jump   **Jump** means to go off the ground and be in the air for a short time. The frog **jumped** into the water. Basketball players **jump** high to try to get the ball. **—jumps, jumped, jumping.**

jungle   A **jungle** is a hot place where a lot of big trees and plants grow. Many kinds of wild animals live in a **jungle**, such as monkeys.

just   1. **Just** means right before. I had **just** gotten home from school when my friend called.
2. Just also means exactly. This dress is **just** my size.
3. Just can also mean only. I'll be done in **just** a minute. We almost won the game. We **just** lost by one point.

journals   A **journal** is a book in which you write down the things that are important to you. The word <u>journal</u> comes from the French word for "day." In a journal, you write what happens each day. Another book of this kind is a **diary**. (<u>Diary</u> also means "day," but in Latin, not French.) If you keep a journal or diary, you put down your feelings and thoughts. You can write every day or less often. What makes a journal are these three things: It is up to date (you write about today or yesterday). It is personal (you give your own ideas). It is friendly and relaxed.

K k

a b c d e f g h i j **k** l m n o p q r s t u v w x y z

keep 1. If you **keep** something, you hold it or save it. I found a pretty rock on the beach. I'm going to **keep** it. In soccer, you try to **keep** the ball away from the other team.
2. **Keep** also means to go on with something. If you **keep** trying, you'll get it right.
—**keeps, kept, keeping.**

kept We **kept** quiet while the baby was asleep. **Kept** is a form of the word KEEP.

key A **key** is a piece of metal with a special shape. It is used to open or close a lock. People use **keys** to open the doors of their cars and homes.

kick To **kick** something means to hit it hard with your foot. Jill can **kick** a soccer ball farther than anyone else in her class.

kid **Kid** is a word used to talk about a child or a young person. You can say "kid" when you talk to your friends, but when you write it is better to say "child" or "boy" or "girl."

kill To **kill** is to make a thing die. Lions **kill** other animals that they hunt for food.

kind 1. Someone who is **kind** is nice to other people and does things to help them. It was **kind** of Michael to visit Mrs. Brown when she was in the hospital.
2. **Kind** also means a group of things that are alike. I want to get a book for Judy. What **kind** of books does she like to read?

kindergarten **Kindergarten** is a grade in school. It comes before first grade. **Kindergarten** is the first class in regular school.

king   A **king** rules over a country. A man becomes **king** because his father was a **king** or his mother was a queen.

A painting of King Arthur, a make-believe **king** who is famous in stories.

kiss   To **kiss** is to touch with the lips. People **kiss** to show they like or love each other. I **kiss** Mom and Dad good-bye when I go to school in the morning.

kitchen   A **kitchen** is a room where food is kept and cooked.

kitten   A **kitten** is a baby cat.

knee   Your **knee** is part of your leg. It is in the middle where your leg bends.

knew   I **knew** that it was Jimmy on the telephone, even though he tried to make his voice sound funny. **Knew** is a form of the word KNOW.

knife   A **knife** is a tool used for cutting. It has a handle and a flat piece of metal with a sharp side. **Knives** are used to cut meat and other food.

knock   **Knock** means to hit hard against something. If you **knock** on a door, you hit it with your hand. Jeff waved his arm and **knocked** over his glass of milk. —**knocks, knocked, knocking.**

knot   A **knot** is a way to tie two things together. You make a **knot** when you tie your shoes.

know   1. If you **know** a thing, you have it in your mind and are sure of it. I got this book for my dad. I **know** he likes books about baseball. I've seen that boy in school, but I don't **know** his name. How long have you and Jennie **known** each other? 2. **Know** also means to be able to do something. My little brother already **knows** how to ride a two-wheel bike. —**knows, knew, known, knowing.**

L l

ladder   A **ladder** is a thing you use to climb up or down.

lady   **Lady** is a word that people sometimes use for a woman.

laid   Mom **laid** my clean clothes out on the bed. **Laid** is a form of the word LAY.

lake   A **lake** is a place with a lot of water. A **lake** has land around it on all sides.

lamp   A **lamp** is a thing that gives out light. **Lamps** now use electricity to make light. Older **lamps** used to use oil.

land   The ground we live on is called the **land**. The earth has water and **land** on it. That **land** is too dry to grow grass on. When an airplane comes down from the air, it **lands** on the ground.

language   The words that people speak and write are called a **language**. This book is written in the English **language**.

large   When something is **large**, it is big. The elephant is a very **large** animal. It is **larger** than any other animal on land.

last   **1.** When a thing comes at the end, it is **last**. The **last** one is after everything else. 'Z' is the **last** letter in the alphabet.
2. Last also means at a time before now. The ground is wet. It must have rained **last** night.

late   **1.** You are **late** when you are not at a place by the right time. He got to the bus stop too **late.** His bus had already left.
2. Late is a time that is not early. On Friday night Bobby got to stay up **late** to watch a movie.

later   When a thing happens after something else, it is **later**. Ben gets to stay up **later** than his little brother does.

laugh   A **laugh** is a sound you make when you feel good. People **laugh** when something is funny or when they are happy. We all **laughed** at the silly things the dog was doing.

laundry   Dirty clothes that need to be washed are **laundry**.

law   A **law** is a rule that tells you what you can or cannot do. The government makes **laws** for a country or a state. It is against the **law** to drive a car too fast. A **lawyer** is a person whose work has to do with the law.

lay   1. **Lay** means to put a thing down on a place. You can **lay** your books on that table.
2. **Lay** is also a past form of the word LIE. The baby **lay** down and took a nap.

lazy   If you are **lazy**, you don't want to do any work. I felt **lazy** and stayed in bed until noon.

lead   To **lead** means to go first and show the way. I will **lead** you to my secret hiding place. This word sounds like "need." Someone who **leads** is a **leader.**

lead   **Lead** is a name for a heavy black metal. This word sounds like "head" or "bed."

leaf   A **leaf** is a green part that grows out from a plant.

league   A group of sports teams that play each other is a **league.**

learn   When you get to know about a thing, you **learn** it. Last year I **learned** to ride a bike. (See the box on this page.)

least   The **least** is the smallest amount. A penny is worth the **least** of any U.S. coin. I didn't win, but **at least** I played well.

learn/teach   People sometimes get mixed up about **learn** and **teach.** Both these words are called **verbs.** Both words mean that you get to know how to do something. "I want to learn to throw a football. I hope my brother will teach me how to do it." Notice the difference with teach. It has another word with it, me. This word is called the **object** of the verb teach. An object is a word that comes after the verb. The verb tells what happens. Then the object tells who, or what, it happens to. My brother will teach me.

leave When you go away from a place or a thing, you **leave** it. Dad **leaves** the house at 7:00 each morning to go to work. I have too much to carry, so I'm going to **leave** this bag here. **—leaves, left, leaving.**

leaves Gary picked up all the **leaves** in the yard. **Leaves** means more than one LEAF.

led The first-grade teacher **led** her students out to play. **Led** is a form of the word LEAD.

left The **left** is one side of a thing. The other side is the RIGHT. The driver of a car sits on the **left**.

left I **left** my book at school and had to go back to get it. **Left** is a form of the word LEAVE.

leg A **leg** is a part of your body. **Legs** are used for walking and running. People have two **legs**. Many animals have four **legs**.

lemon A **lemon** is a yellow fruit with a sour taste. We use **lemons** to make **lemonade.**

less A smaller amount or not as much of a thing is **less**. Five is **less** than six. The job was easy. I was done in **less** than an hour.

lesson A **lesson** is something you learn. Today we had a math **lesson** on feet and inches. Julie is taking **lessons** to learn how to be a dancer.

let To **let** something happen is to say it is all right for it to happen. Mom **let** us each have another glass of apple juice.

let's **Let's** is a shorter way to say or write "let us." **Let's** go over to the park and play ball.

letter **1.** A **letter** is a part of the alphabet. We use **letters** to write words. A, B, and C are **letters**. **2.** A **letter** is a thing you write and send to someone else.

letters There are rules to follow when you write a **letter.** You start by writing the date as the **heading** in the top right corner of the page. Then you move down and to the left and write "Dear ———," (the name of the person you are writing to). Then you write what is called the **body** of the letter. This is the main part, with your message. You end the letter with a **closing** such as "Yours truly," "Your friend," or "Love." (Choose a closing that fits the person you are writing to.) Then you sign your name. The **closing** and **signature** lines go on the right.

library A **library** is a place where many books are kept. You can go to a public **library** and borrow books to read at home.

lie When you make yourself flat on something, you **lie** on it. You **lie** down on a bed to go to sleep.
—**lies, lay, lain, lying.**

lie If you say something that is not true, you **lie**. He broke the toy and then **lied** by saying he didn't do it.
—**lies, lied, lying.**

life A thing that has **life** is alive. It can breathe, grow, take in food, and move. People, plants, and animals all have **life**. The time when you are alive is called your **lifetime.**

lift When you pick something up, you **lift** it. Nancy **lifted** the baby off the floor and held him in her arms.

light When a thing is not dark, it is **light**. During the day, there is **light** from the sun. Lamps and fires give off **light**. White and yellow are **light** colors. Put on a **light** so that we can see.
—**lights, lit** or **lighted, lighting.**

light When a thing is **light**, it is not heavy. An egg is **light**, but a rock the same size is heavy. A balloon is **light**.

lightning **Lightning** is a bright, quick line of light across the sky. **Lightning** comes with thunder during a storm.

Lightning flashes across the summer sky.

like To **like** a thing is to feel good about it. Most children **like** ice cream. Joan is a friend of mine and I **like** to be with her.

like If one thing is the same as or close to another, it is **like** it. She looks **like** her mom. They have the same color hair and eyes. "May" sounds **like** "day."

line A **line** is long and thin. Paper to write on usually has **lines** on it. People were in a long **line** waiting to go into the movie.

lion A **lion** is a large animal. **Lions** are part of the cat family.

lions In the picture, the male lion is at the top and the female is below.

liquid A **liquid** is something wet like water, milk, juice, or oil.

list A **list** is a group of things put down on paper. Dad made a **list** to help him remember what foods to buy at the store.

listen When you **listen**, you are trying to hear something. Dad **listens** to music on his car radio. The teacher told us to **listen** carefully to what he said.

little **Little** means not very big. It means the same thing as "small." Babies are **little**.

live **1.** To **live** is to have LIFE. People, animals, and plants **live**. Things like rocks, chairs, and cars don't **live**.
2. Your home is where you **live**. My cousins **live** in New York. Deer **live** in fields and woods.

load A **load** is the amount that can be carried. The driver put a **load** of boxes on his truck. We **loaded** the books into the car.

lock A **lock** is a thing that keeps something shut. Most **locks** open with a key. We **lock** the doors to our house when we go out.

log A **log** is a big, thick piece of wood. People burn **logs** in a fire.

long When a thing is **long,** it is far from one end to the other. A giraffe has a **long** neck. It takes a **long** time to fly from New York to California.

look When you try to see something, you **look**. **Look** at that pretty new dress Mom has on. James was **looking** in his closet for his baseball glove.

loose When a thing is going to come out or off, it is **loose**. The little boy had a **loose** tooth that was about to fall out.

lose **1.** When you **lose** a thing, you don't have it and you don't know where it is. Henry didn't want to **lose** his lunch money, so he gave it to the teacher to hold.
2. When you don't win, you **lose**. We're behind 1-0. If we don't get a goal now, we'll **lose** the game. If you lose, that is called a **loss.**

lost Yesterday, Kenny **lost** his jacket. He thinks he left it at the park. **Lost** is a form of the word LOSE.

lot A **lot** means a big number or amount. A **lot** of students go to this school. Kara likes to put **lots** of salt on her food and Mom says she shouldn't.

loud Something **loud** makes lots of noise and can be heard for a long way. The jet plane made a very **loud** noise as it flew by us.

love When you **love** someone, you like that person very, very much. Parents and their children **love** each other.

low **1.** When a thing is **low,** it is close to the ground. Cars can go under that bridge, but it's too **low** for big trucks.
2. Low also means there is not a big number or amount. We haven't had any rain, and the lake is very **low.** Five dollars is a **low** price for a shirt.

luck **Luck** is when something happens that you didn't expect. Carolyn had good **luck** and found a dollar on the street. It was bad **luck** that it rained for our beach party. A thing that is **lucky** brings good **luck.** We won our game against the best team. This was our **lucky** day.

lunch **Lunch** is the food that you eat in the middle of the day.

-ly words "He's a slow worker. He works slowly." "Suzie is a good friend. She's very friendly." Can you see the way these words change? Slow becomes slow**ly**. Friend becomes friend**ly**. They add **ly** at the end. This **ly** ending is a **suffix.** (We say this as "SUFF-iks.") The meaning of a word does not really change when a suffix is added. Slow and slowly both mean "not fast." Friend and friendly both tell about someone who is nice. But the suffix can make a new word. Letters can go on the front of a word, too. That is called a **prefix.** Luck can add the suffix **y** to make lucky. Then it can add the prefix **un** to make unlucky ("not lucky").

M m

a b c d e f g h i j k l m n o p q r s t u v w x y z

machine   A **machine** is a thing that does work for people. It has parts that move. Clothes were once made by hand, but now they are made by **machines.**

mad   If you are **mad,** you feel bad and upset about something. Sarah got **mad** at Mark when he hit her with a snowball.

made   I didn't buy this dress in a store. My Mom **made** it. **Made** is a form of the word MAKE.

magazine   A **magazine** is a thing to read. It has stories and also pictures. 'Time' **Magazine** gives news of the world every week.

magic   **Magic** is a way to make something look real that is not. She did a **magic** trick by pulling a rabbit out of a hat. A person who uses **magic** is a **magician**.

mail   Letters that are sent from one place to another are called **mail.** Dad **mailed** a birthday present to our Grandma in Florida. The place that sends the **mail** is called the **post office.**

main   The **main** thing is the most important thing. The big road that goes through the middle of our city is called **Main** Street.

make   If you **make** something, you cause it to become real. That company **makes** TV sets. Don't **make** so much noise or the baby will wake up. Mom is **making** sandwiches for lunch. **—makes, made, making.**

make-believe   **Make-believe** is something that is not real. "Peter Pan" is a **make-believe** story about a boy who can fly.

male   A **male** is a boy or a man. A **male** lion has long hair on its head, but a female lion doesn't.

man   When a boy grows up, he's called a **man**. Dad often rides to work with two other **men.**

many   **Many** means a large number or amount. Dinosaurs lived on earth **many** years ago.

map   A **map** is a drawing that shows where different places are. Dad looked at the **map** to see which road we should take.

march   People **march** when they walk together in the same way.

mark   **1.** A **mark** is something you can see on a place. The teacher **marked** an 'X' on my paper next to the wrong answer. **2.** A **mark** tells how well you did in school. Sue got a **mark** of 100 on her math test.

marry   A husband and wife are **married** to each other. This is called a **marriage**.

mask   A **mask** is something you use to hide your face. I wore a **mask** to school on Halloween.

match   **1.** When things **match**, they are the same. These socks don't **match.** One is black and the other one is gray. **2.** A **match** is a thin piece of wood or paper. **Matches** can be lit to make a fire.

math   **Math** is the study of numbers. 2+2 is a form of **math. Math** is short for **mathematics.**

matter   If someone says "what's the **matter**," they're asking what is wrong. What's the **matter** with Toni? Why is she crying?

may   A thing that **may** happen is not sure to happen, but it could happen. We **may** go to the beach today, if it stops raining.

maybe   **Maybe** means that a thing may happen, or may be true. I don't know who sent me this card. **Maybe** it was Melissa, because it looks like her writing.

married   To tell about what happened before, you add **ed** to a word. "Mrs. Sims marked 'OK' on my paper." "The soldiers marched off to war." "Mom and Dad got married in 1969." Do you see how married is different from marked and marched? Those words just add **ed.** Married changes the **y** in marry to **i,** and then adds **ed.** Words that end in **y** change this way when they add **ed** or **s.** (Marry also becomes marries.)

meanings If a word did not **mean** anything, it would be be just noise in the air or scratches on paper. <u>Rain</u> is four letters that mean "sky water" or "water falling from clouds." What do <u>raik</u> or <u>tain</u> mean? Nothing.

All people who use English share the same words. We agree on what these words mean. We use <u>blue</u> to mean a color. We don't use it to mean "a kind of tree" or "to go very fast." Each word has its own meaning. A dictionary tells you what these meanings are.

me   **Me** means that something happens to "I." I asked Mom to give **me** to a ride to the park.

meal   A **meal** is a time when people eat. Lunch is the **meal** we eat in the middle of the day.

mean   **1.** A person who is **mean** is not nice. We all like Andy because he never acts **mean**. **2. Mean** can show that two things are the same. A red light **means** that you have to stop. The **meaning** of a word is the way people use and understand it. —**means, meant, meaning.**

measure   When you **measure** a thing, you find out how big it is. Sally grew two inches since the last time she **measured** herself.

meat   **Meat** is food that comes from animals. **Meat** from a cow is **beef. Pork** is from a pig.

medicine   **Medicine** is what you take to feel better if you are sick.

meet   **Meet** means to come up to and see a person. Dad came to school to **meet** my teacher. The city had a **meeting** to talk about building a new park. —**meets, met, meeting.**

memory   Your **memory** is the way you remember things. Mom can name every person who was in her high school class. She has a good **memory.**

men   **Men** means "more than one man." There are eleven **men** on a football team.

mess   If a place is a **mess**, it is dirty and things are not where they should be. I have to clean up the **mess** in my room.

message   A **message** is words sent by one person to another. It can be in a letter or a note.

met   At the store we **met** the man who lives next door to us. **Met** is a form of the word MEET.

metal A **metal** is hard and it is found in the ground. It can be used to make things. Iron, silver, and lead are **metals.**

meter A **meter** is a way to tell how long a thing is. A **meter** is a little more than three feet. In other countries people measure with **meters** instead of with feet.

middle A thing that is in the **middle** is not on either side. It is between the two sides. To start a soccer game, you put the ball in the **middle** of the field and kick it. Twelve o'clock noon is in the **middle** of the day.

might **Might** means that a thing may happen. It's getting dark out. I think it **might** rain.

mile A **mile** is a way to show how long a thing is. There are 5,280 feet in a **mile**. Lee walks a **mile** to school every day. The car was going 25 **miles** an hour.

milk **Milk** is something to drink. It is white, and it comes from cows and other animals.

million A **million** is a very large number. One **million** is written as 1,000,000. There are **millions** of stars in the sky.

mind 1. The **mind** is the part of a person that thinks. You use your **mind** to learn and to remember things.
2. **Mind** means to care about a thing. Do you **mind** if I change the TV to another show?

mine That red pencil is hers, but this blue one is **mine**.

minus **Minus** is a word we use to take away one number from another. Five **minus** three is two.

minute A **minute** is a way to measure time. A **minute** is 60 seconds long. There are 60 **minutes** in one hour.

mirror A **mirror** is a smooth piece of glass that you can see yourself in.

miss 1. When you **miss** a thing, you don't hit it or get it. Eddie **missed** the ball and it rolled past him and went down the hill.
2. **Miss** means to feel sad that you're not with someone you like. Angela **missed** her Dad when he was away on a trip.

Miss **Miss** is used before the name of a woman who is not married. "Mrs. Jean Dow and her daughter **Miss** Mary Dow."

mistake If you do a thing the wrong way, it is a **mistake**. Jimmy made a spelling **mistake** in his story. He wrote "alot" instead of "a lot."

mix **Mix** means to put things together. You **mix** lemon juice with sugar and water to make a drink called lemonade.

model A **model** is a small copy of something. Dad gave me a **model** car for my birthday.

modern If a thing is **modern**, it is new and up to date. The jet plane and the computer are **modern** inventions.

moment A **moment** is a very short time. She stopped her car the **moment** the boy ran into the street in front of her.

Monday **Monday** is a day of the week. **Monday** comes after Sunday and before Tuesday.

money **Money** is what we use to buy things. Quarters and dollar bills are **money**.

monkey A **monkey** is a small animal with long, thin arms and a very long tail. **Monkeys** live in trees.

monster A **monster** is a big, ugly animal found in stories. **Monsters** are not real.

month A **month** is one of the 12 parts of a year. The 12 **months** of the year are **January, February, March, April, May, June, July, August, September, October, November,** and **December.**

mood A **mood** is the way a person feels. She is in a really bad **mood** today and keeps shouting at everyone.

moon The **moon** is the large, round body that you can see in the night sky. The **moon** moves around the earth.

monkey These are three different kinds of **monkeys.**

75

more **More** is a larger number or amount. **More** is the opposite of less. New York has **more** people than any other city in the U. S. Todd was still hungry, and asked for some **more** meat.

morning **Morning** is the early part of the day. It comes after the night and before the afternoon.

most If you have **most** of a thing, you have nearly all of it. **Most** of the people in our class are going on the trip. Twenty are going, and four are not going.

mother A **mother** is a woman who has a child or children. Children call their **mother** Mom or Mommy.

motor A **motor** is a machine that makes things work. A washing machine uses a **motor** to make the clothes go around.

motorcycle A **motorcycle** is like a bicycle, but it is bigger and heavier. It has a motor and can go on roads like a car.

mountain A **mountain** is a place that is very high up. **Mountains** are like hills, but they are much higher.

mouse A **mouse** is a small animal. A **mouse** has soft fur, a pointed nose, and a long thin tail. The word for more than one **mouse** is **mice.**

mouth Your **mouth** is the opening in your face where you put food in when you eat. Your teeth and **tongue** are inside your **mouth.**

move **Move** means to go from one place to another. Dad asked Cathy to **move** her books off the table because it was time for dinner. Jeff used to live on my street, but he **moved** to Texas. —**moves, moved, moving.**

movie A **movie** is a story put into moving pictures that you watch. People can see **movies** at a **movie theater** or on television.

mountain This is Mount McKinley, the highest **mountain** in North America.

Mr./Mister "<u>Mister</u> Wilson lives next door to us. I always see <u>Mr.</u> Wilson out working in the yard." It's the same man, but the name is a bit different. **Mr.** is a shorter way to write **Mister. Mr.** is what is called an **abbreviation.** (We say it as "uh-bree-vee-AY-shun.") An abbreviation is a short way to write a longer word.

      Notice the period at the end of **Mr.** Abbreviations are followed by a period to show that some letters have been left out. For example, <u>United States</u> is abbreviated as U. S. <u>Friday</u> is abbreviated Fri.

Mr. **Mr.** is used before the name of a man. **Mr.** is short for **Mister.** (See the box on this page.)

Mrs. **Mrs.** is used before the name of a woman who is married. "**Mrs.** Jean Dow and her daughter Miss Mary Dow."

Ms. **Ms.** is used before the name of a woman. It does not show whether the woman is married or not married.

much **Much** is a lot of a thing. She was sick yesterday, but she feels **much** better today. I put too **much** milk in the glass and it ran over the top.

mud **Mud** is soft, wet dirt. A place that has mud is **muddy.**

multiply **Multiply** means to add a number to itself a certain number of times. To **multiply** 5 by 3 is the same as 5 + 5 + 5.

muscle A **muscle** is part of your body under the skin. **Muscles** make the body move.

museum A **museum** is a place where interesting things are shown. Our City **Museum** has pictures and other kinds of art.

music **Music** is a group of beautiful sounds put together. Our family saw a **musical** play with many songs and dances.

must If you **must** do something, you have to do it. People **must** have water to live.

my I have to clean **my** room after dinner. I'm going to do it all by **myself.**

mystery A **mystery** is a thing that is hard to know about and understand. This book is a **mystery** story about how a famous painting was stolen.

N n

a b c d e f g h i j k l m n o p q r s t u v w x y z

nail **1.** A **nail** is a sharp, thin piece of metal. **Nails** are used to hold pieces of wood together. **2.** A **nail** is a hard piece on the end of a finger or toe.

name A **name** is what a thing is called. My teacher's **name** is Mrs. Burns. The **name** of this flower is the rose. Kim has a dog **named** 'Prince.'

nap When you sleep for a short time, you take a **nap**.

nature **Nature** is everything in the world that was not made by people. Plants, animals, oceans, and mountains are all part of **nature**.

near When something is close by, it is **near**. Our house is **near** the park and I play ball there a lot. It is now **nearly** nine o'clock.

neck Your **neck** is part of your body. Your **neck** is between your head and shoulders. A giraffe has a very long **neck**.

need When you must have something, you **need** it. Plants **need** water to stay alive. This box is really heavy. I **need** some help carrying it. Jerry **needs** a quiet place to do his homework. **—needs, needed, needing.**

neighbor A person who lives near by is a **neighbor**. When we moved in to our new house, the **neighbors** came over to meet us. A group of houses on a street or block is called a **neighborhood**.

neither Not one, and not the other, is **neither.** My sister didn't like the movie, and **neither** did I. We both thought it was really silly.

nest A **nest** is a place where a bird lays its eggs. Birds build **nests** from grass, mud, and other things.

nest The **nest** of a meadowlark.

never **Never** means not ever or not at any time. That was the first time I ever flew on a plane. I had **never** been on one before. Mom told us **never** to run out in the street without looking.

new When something has just been done or made, it is **new**. Laurie got a **new** bike for her birthday. That's a **new** TV show that just started this week.

news The **news** is the story of things that happen each day. Mom and Dad watch the **news** on TV. The teacher read us a **news** story about our town.

newspaper A **newspaper** is a paper that tells about the news. A **newspaper** also has pictures and other things in it.

next The one that comes after this one is **next**. The new store will open **next** month. Lisa was first in line, and Mike was **next**.

nice Something **nice** makes you feel happy. It was such a **nice** day that we played outside all day. I think Mrs. Peters is the **nicest** teacher in our school.

nickel A **nickel** is a coin. One **nickel** is the same as five cents.

night **Night** is when it is dark outside. **Night** is the time when it is not day.

no 1. **No** means "not yes." You say **no** when something can't be or you don't want it to be. **No**, I can't play now. I'm doing my homework. Would you like a glass of milk? **No**, thank you. 2. **No** means not any or not at all. You can't have a sandwich. There is **no** bread left.

nobody **Nobody** means no person or not anyone. **Nobody** lives in that old house. **Nobody** in the class knew the answer.

noise   A **noise** is a loud sound. The **noise** from the thunder woke me up. Something that makes lots of **noise** is **noisy.**

none   **None** means not one or not any. **None** of the stores were open on Sunday night. I waited for a bus, but **none** came by.

noon   Twelve o'clock in the day is **noon.**

north   **North** is a direction on the earth. Canada is **north** of the United States.

nose   Your **nose** is a part of your face. You use your **nose** to smell things and to breathe.

not   **Not** means in no way. My book was **not** where I left it. I guess someone took it. Bluegrass is **not** really blue. It is green.

note   A **note** is a short letter. Dad had to write a **note** to the teacher saying why I missed school.

nothing   **Nothing** means no thing or things. I ate all my dinner. There was **nothing** left on my plate.

notice   When you see a thing and think about it, you **notice** it. Did you **notice** that Jan has a new haircut?

now   **Now** is at this time or right away. I was born in New York, but **now** I live in Texas. Dad wants you to come home **now.**

number   A **number** is used to count things. **Numbers** stand for how many things there are. The **number** of students in our class is 30.

nurse   A **nurse** is a person whose job is to take care of sick people. Many **nurses** work in hospitals. Others work in doctors' offices.

nut   A **nut** is a thing to eat. **Nuts** grow on trees. A **nut** has a hard shell outside and a seed inside.

nouns   Which animals can you see at the zoo? You can see lions, tigers, and elephants. The words lion, tiger, and elephant are the names of animals. These words are called **nouns.** Nouns name things. A **noun** is a word that names a person, animal, place, or thing.

The words doctor, teacher, and sister name people. They are all nouns. Lake, house, and office are nouns that name places. Book, toy, and apple are nouns that name things. Some nouns stand for things that cannot be seen, such as music, subject, and idea.

80

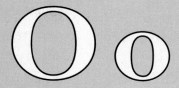

O o

a b c d e f g h i j k l m n O p q r s t u v w x y z

oak An **oak** is a big tree. **Acorns** are nuts that grow on **oak** trees.

obey To **obey** is to do what someone tells you to do. When the teacher asked the children to line up, they all **obeyed** her.

object An **object** is a real thing that you can see and touch. A desk is an **object** that can have other **objects** like books, paper, and pencils on it.

ocean An **ocean** is a very large area of salt water. Much of the planet Earth is covered by four great **oceans:** the Pacific **Ocean,** the Atlantic **Ocean,** the Indian **Ocean,** and the Arctic **Ocean.**

o'clock **O'clock** is a word that is used to say what time it is. Our family usually eats dinner at six **o'clock.**

odd **1.** Something **odd** is strange or unusual. The telephone keeps ringing, but when I answer it there's no one there. That's **odd.** **2. Odd** numbers like 1, 3, 5, 7, and 9 cannot be divided in half the way even numbers can.

of The shape **of** a circle is round. I drank a glass **of** water. We live in the state **of** Texas.

off Jim took **off** his coat. The wind blew the papers **off** the table. Please turn **off** the radio.

office An **office** is a building or other place where people go to work. My mother works in a doctor's **office.**

officer A person who leads soldiers in the army is an **officer.** A policeman is called a police **officer.**

often   If a thing happens **often,** it happens again and again. We **often** go to play in the park. Winter nights are **often** cold.

oil   Oil is a thick liquid. The **oil** that cars use comes from the earth. Other **oils** from plants or animals are used in cooking.

OK   **OK** is another way to say all right or "yes." I asked Mom if I could go outside to play, and she said **OK.** When Matt fell down, his dad asked if he was **OK.**

old   **1. Old** means not new or young. That's a very **old** house. It was built 200 years ago. The story was about an **old** man and his grandson.
2. Your age is how **old** you are. Sharon will be seven years **old** on her next birthday.

on   The plates for dinner are already **on** the table. Our family went **on** a trip. Patty put her coat **on.** Please turn **on** the lights.

once   **Once** means one time. Your birthday comes only **once** a year.

one   **One** is the word for the number **1. One** is the number between zero and two.

only   **1.** When there is just one of a thing, it is the **only** one. Lee was the **only** person in the class who could answer the question. **2. Only** can also mean a small number. Rosa's little sister is **only** three years old.

open   Something **open** is not closed. I want to buy a book. Is the bookstore **open** today? She **opened** the door and went out.

opposite   The **opposite** of a thing is not like it at all. "Hot" is the **opposite** of "cold."

or   The word **or** is used to choose between two things. Do you want milk **or** juice with lunch?

orange   An **orange** is a round fruit. **Orange** is also the name of the color of this fruit.

Oranges, with the flower seen above.

order Order means that one thing is placed after another in a certain way. A, B, C, D is a kind of order. So is 1,2,3,4. When you use words, order is important too. A sentence you write should have the words in the correct order. First in order is the **subject.** The subject tells what the sentence is about: "Cats." Then comes the **verb.** The verb tells what the subject is, or what it does: "eat mice." **Subject-verb** is the correct **word order** for a sentence: "Cats eat mice." If you changed the word order, you would change the meaning: "Mice eat cats." Is that right?

order 1. An **order** is something that you tell someone to do. A soldier in the army must follow his officer's **orders.**
2. **Order** is also the way things are placed. The girls lined up in alphabetical **order** by last name. (See the box on this page.)

other The **other** thing is not this thing. You carry this box. I'll take the **other** one. Roberto is taller than all the **other** boys in his class.

ounce An **ounce** is an amount that something can weigh. An **ounce** is very light. There are 16 **ounces** in one pound.

our **Our** means that we have it. We all went for a ride in **our** new car. That white car is **ours.**

out Something **out** is not in. It's raining **out,** so we can't go **out** to play. The sun came **out** from behind a big cloud.

outdoors **Outdoors** is any place that is not inside a building. Baseball is played **outdoors.**

outside The **outside** is what is not inside. The dog sat **outside** the door, waiting to come in. The weather **outside** was cold, but the house was warm.

oven An **oven** is a thing you put things in to cook. Mom put the cake in the **oven** for one hour.

over 1. **Over** means above. I hung the picture **over** my bed.
2. **Over** also means finished. When the movie was **over,** the lights came back on.
3. **Over** can also mean again. Paula lost her homework paper, so she had to do the work **over.**

own If you **own** a thing, it is yours. Who **owns** that cat that I always see around here? Tara was in a room with her sister, but now she has her **own** room.

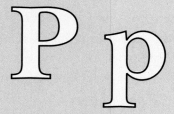

P p

a b c d e f g h i j k l m n o p q r s t u v w x y z

package   A **package** is a box. We got a big **package** from my Grandma in the mail today.

page   A **page** is one side of a piece of paper. Newspapers and magazines have **pages**. You are now on **page** 84 of your book.

paid   Bruce **paid** ten dollars to buy his new shirt. **Paid** is a form of the word PAY.

pain   When a part of your body hurts, you feel **pain**. Joyce had a **pain** in her stomach because she ate too fast.

paint   **Paint** is a way to give color to things. **Paint** is wet as it goes on. It dries to keep the color on. Maria **painted** a picture of her house. A picture that is painted is a **painting**. A person who paints something is a **painter.**

pair   A **pair** is a set of two things that are the same. Shoes and socks come in **pairs.**

pan   A **pan** is a thing to cook food in. Most **pans** are wide and low with a flat bottom. Mom cooked the pie in a round **pan**.

pants   **Pants** are a kind of clothes that you wear to cover your legs.

paper   **Paper** is something to write on. **Paper** is made from wood that is made into very thin, flat pieces. The pages of a book are made of **paper**.

parent   A **parent** is a mother or father. **Parents** are men and women who have children.

park   A **park** is a place to play or rest. **Parks** have trees and grass. Some have fields to play ball.

part A **part** is one piece of a bigger thing. The heart is a **part** of your body. New York State is **part** of the United States.

party A **party** is when people get together to have a good time. Megan's friends all had fun at her birthday **party**.

pass **1.** To **pass** means to go by. The car pulled out and **passed** another car that was going slow. **2.** When you hand or throw a thing to someone, you **pass** it. Please **pass** me the butter. Joe **passed** the football up the field.

past **1.** The **past** is the time that has gone by. The **past** is before now. In the **past**, people had to walk or ride horses, because there were no cars. **2.** When a thing goes by, it goes **past**. My friend waved to me as his car went **past** our house.

path A **path** is a place to walk. We took the **path** to the river.

pattern A **pattern** is the way that colors, shapes, and lines go together. The American flag has a **pattern** of stars and stripes.

pay When you give money to get something, you **pay** for it. I had to **pay** for my bus ticket. —**pays, paid, paying.**

pea A **pea** is a vegetable. **Peas** are small, round, and green.

peace When there is no war or fighting, there is **peace**.

peanut A **peanut** is something to eat. **Peanuts** are seeds that look and taste like nuts. They are eaten whole or made into **peanut butter**.

pen A **pen** is a thing that you can write or draw with. **Pens** have a liquid inside called **ink**.

pencil A **pencil** is a thing that you can write or draw with. **Pencils** are made of wood.

past-time verbs "I walked home." Does that tell you when the walk happened? Yes, it does. It happened some time before now. It could be an hour before or a year before. The time before now is the **past**. The word walked is a **past-time verb.** How do you know that "I walked home" tells about the past? You know by the letters **ed** at the end of walk**ed**. Most past-time verbs end with **ed**. Be careful, though. Some verbs do not add **ed** to tell about the past. These verbs change spelling instead. Some examples are run-**ran**, go-**went**, do-**did**, and see-**saw**.

penny A **penny** is a metal coin. One **penny** is the same as one **cent.** One hundred **pennies** make one dollar.

people When there is more than one person, we say **people.** A lot of **people** came to watch the football game.

pepper **Pepper** is a thing to put on food to make it taste better. **Pepper** has a hot, sharp taste.

perfect Something **perfect** has nothing wrong with it. Luis got every word right on his spelling test. He had a **perfect** paper.

perhaps **Perhaps** is another word for maybe. **Perhaps** it will rain today, and **perhaps** not.

period A **period** is a small dot like this . that goes at the end of a sentence. There is a **period** after these words. (See the box on this page.)

person A **person** is one man, one woman, or one child. The last **person** to go to bed should turn out all the lights. A chair is a seat for one **person.**

pet A **pet** is an animal that people like to keep in their house with them. Dogs and cats are **pets.**

phone **Phone** is a shorter word for TELEPHONE. My **phone** number is 546-8713.

piano **Pianos** make music. A **piano** has a row of small black and white blocks called **keys.** If you push a key, it causes the **piano** to make a musical sound.

pick **1.** When you **pick** a thing, you choose it. Dad **picked** out a book to read on his plane trip. **2.** When you take a thing in your hands, you **pick** it up. Alice **picked** up the ball and threw it to her friend.

periods This is a **period .** It is also called a "full stop." You can think of it as being like a stop sign on the road. When you come to a stop sign, you stop for a short time, and then go on. A period works the same way in writing. It stops, or ends, a sentence. "I stopped by your house **.** But no one was home."

Another sign is the **comma.** This is a comma **,** . A comma means "slow down," not "stop." It cannot end a sentence. You can't write, "I stopped by your house **,** But no one was home." You'd have to make it into one sentence: "I stopped by your house **,** but no one was home."

86

picture   A **picture** is something that shows what a person or a thing looks like. The students drew **pictures** to go with their stories. Mary took my **picture** with her new camera.

pie   A **pie** is something to eat for dessert. Inside most **pies** is fruit or something sweet.

piece   1. A **piece** is one part of a bigger thing. Rachel gave me a **piece** of her apple.
2. A **piece** is one of a group of things. David wrote his name on a **piece** of paper.

pig   A **pig** is an animal. A **pig** has a fat round body, four legs, and a short tail. **Pigs** are kept on farms and used as food.

pig   A **pig** can also be called a **hog.**

pile   A **pile** is many things of the same kind on top of each other. They put the wood in a big **pile.**

pill   A **pill** is a thing to take when you are sick.

pillow   A **pillow** is something soft to put under your head when you lie down or sleep.

pilot   A **pilot** is a person who flies an airplane. The **pilot** landed the plane on the ground.

pin   A **pin** is a very thin piece of metal with a sharp point. **Pins** hold things together. Dean **pinned** his paper up on the wall.

pink   **Pink** is a color that is part red and part white.

pint   A **pint** is an amount of liquid. One **pint** is the same as 16 ounces. There are two **pints** in one quart.

pipe   A **pipe** is a long, straight thing made of metal, glass, or plastic. **Pipes** carry water, gas, and other things from one place to another.

pitch   To **pitch** is to throw a baseball. The player who does this is called the **pitcher.**

pizza   **Pizza** is something to eat. **Pizzas** are pies with tomatoes, cheese, and other things on top.

place A **place** is where a person or thing is. The park near our house is a good **place** to play. Grandpa went back to visit the **place** where he was born.
—**places, placed, placing.**

plan A **plan** is an idea about what to do or how to do it. Our class is making **plans** to have a Halloween party. Katie **plans** to go to soccer camp this summer.
—**plans, planned, planning.**

plane **Plane** is a shorter word for AIRPLANE. We took a **plane** flight from Boston to Chicago.

planet A **planet** is a big, round body in the sky. Nine **planets** move around the sun. We live on the **planet** called Earth. The other **planets** are **Mercury, Venus, Mars, Jupiter, Saturn, Uranus, Neptune,** and **Pluto.**

planet This is the **planet** Saturn.

plant A **plant** is a living thing that is not an animal. Flowers, trees, bushes, and grass are all **plants**. To **plant** a seed is to put it in the ground to make it grow.

plastic Cups, dishes, toys, and many other things are made of **plastic**. When it is hot, **plastic** is soft and easy to make into any shape. When it cools, it is hard.

plate We put food on a **plate** to eat it. **Plates** are round and flat.

play 1. To **play** is to do things for fun. The children **played** on the beach. Let's **play** baseball. If you **play** a game, you are a **player.** 2. To **play** also means to make music. Tina can **play** the piano. 3. A **play** is a story that is acted out on a stage.

playground A **playground** is a place to play outside. Most **playgrounds** have swings, slides, and bars to climb on.

please The word **please** is used to ask for something in a nice way. **Please** pass me the milk.

plenty When there is a lot of a thing, there is **plenty**. Let's leave now, so that we'll have **plenty** of time to get there.

plurals   "They have three children. They have two <u>boy**s**</u> and one <u>girl</u>." Do you see the way the letter **s** is used here? The **s** has the meaning "more than one." There is <u>one</u> girl, no **s**. But there are <u>two</u> boy**s**, with the **s**. A word like <u>girl</u> that means "one of a thing" is called a **singular** word. A word like <u>boy**s**</u> that means "more than one thing" is called a **plural** word. (Say "SING-gyuh-lur" and "PLURE-ull.") Look at the words on this page. <u>Pocket</u> and <u>poem</u> are singular words. <u>Pocket**s**</u> and <u>poem**s**</u> are plural words. The **s** at the end tells you that they are plural.

plus   **Plus** means "and." Three **plus** two is five. The sign **+** means **plus,** as in 3 **+** 2.

pocket   A **pocket** is a small bag inside clothing. People carry money, keys, pencils, and other things in their **pockets**.

poem   A **poem** is a kind of writing that uses words in a special way. In many **poems,** the lines end with words that sound alike, such as "new" and "do." The writing of **poems** is called **poetry.** A person who writes **poems** is a **poet.**

point   **1.** A **point** is the sharp end of something. You write with the **point** of a pencil.
2. When you **point**, you use a finger or stick to show where to look. The teacher **pointed** to the problem on the blackboard.
3. Point can mean the idea of a thing. The **point** of the story was that we need new schools here.

poison   **Poison** is something that can hurt or kill you if it gets in or on your body. The bite of some snakes has **poison** in it. These snakes are **poisonous.**

pole   A **pole** is a long stick or post made of metal or wood. Kyle caught a fish with his new fishing **pole.**

police   The **police** are people whose job is to make sure that other people are safe and do not break the law. **Police officers** wear uniforms and drive in special **police cars.**

polite   When you speak and act in a very nice way, you are being **polite**. Ted tries to be **polite** by saying "please" and "thank you" when he asks for things.

politics   When people try to win elections to be in government, that is **politics.** A person who is in **politics** is a **politician.**

pollute To **pollute** is to put something dirty into the air, water, or earth. Cars **pollute** the air with smoke. **Pollution** is a problem in many big cities.

Pollution hangs over the city of Chicago.

pond A **pond** is water with land around it on all sides. A **pond** is like a lake, only smaller.

pool A **pool** is a thing to swim in. Some **pools** are small and made of plastic. Larger **pools** are dug into the ground. A **pool** is also called a **swimming pool.**

popular If a thing is **popular**, a lot of people like it. "Star Wars" is a very **popular** movie.

poor 1. **Poor** people do not have enough money to buy what they need.
2. **Poor** can also mean bad. Bill got a **poor** grade on the test.

position The **position** of a thing is where it is. In soccer Andy's **position** is right halfback.

possible If a thing can be done, it is **possible**. If it can't be done, it is **impossible.**

post A **post** is a piece of wood or metal that is put in the ground to hold something up.

pot A **pot** is a thing to cook food in. **Pots** are round and deep. I heated up the soup in a **pot.**

potato A **potato** is a vegetable. **Potatoes** are white inside with a brown or red skin. We cook **potatoes** before we eat them.

pound A **pound** is an amount that something can weigh. My little sister weighs 35 **pounds.**

pour When a liquid moves down or out of a place, it **pours**. I **poured** myself a glass of milk. There was a big storm and it was **pouring** rain.

power 1. **Power** is being able to do something. Only humans have the **power** to speak.
2. **Power** makes things work and move. Our stove runs on electric **power.**

practice To **practice** is to do a thing again and again to get better at it. She **practices** playing the piano for an hour every day.

present **1.** The time right now is the **present**. You are reading this book today, in the **present**. **2.** A **present** is a gift. Jody gave me a nice birthday **present**.

president A **president** is the leader of a group of people. George Washington was the first **President** of the U. S.

pretend To **pretend** is to act like something is real when it is not. When he rides in the car, Juan likes to **pretend** he is driving.

pretty Something **pretty** is nice to look at. Sara looks **pretty** in her new dress. I found some **pretty** flowers in the garden.

price The **price** of something is how much it costs. The **price** of that book is three dollars.

prince A **prince** is the son of a king or queen.

princess A **princess** is the daughter of a king or queen. The wife of a prince is also called a **princess**.

principal A **principal** is the person who leads a school.

print To make letters on paper is to **print**. In kindergarten Jimmy learned to **print** his name. The words in this book are **printed** in black letters.

private Something **private** is not for everyone. This is a **private** road. It belongs to the people who own that house.

prize A **prize** is something you win. Lisa got first **prize** in the school Science Fair.

probably If we think a thing will happen, we say **probably**. By the look of those clouds, it will **probably** rain today.

problem **1.** Something that is hard to deal with is a **problem**. Mom went to see the doctor about a **problem** with her back. **2.** A question to answer for school is called a **problem.**

program A **program** is a play or a television show. Mom always watches her favorite TV **program** on Friday nights.

project A piece of work that you do for school is a **project.**

promise If you **promise**, you say that you will really do something. Dad has **promised** to take us to the beach tomorrow.

property A person's **property** belongs to that person. If a man owns a house, it is his **property**.

proud To be **proud** is to feel good about something you have done. Tranh was **proud** of the picture he painted in art class.

prove When you show that something is true, you **prove** it. Anna **proved** that she was a fast runner by winning the race.

public Something **public** is for all the people. Anyone who lives in this town can take books out of the **public** library.

pull To **pull** a thing is to hold it and move it towards you. **Pull** the string and the box will open.

punch To **punch** is to hit very hard with your hand closed.

punish When people do bad things, they may be **punished.** Billy's mother **punished** him because he hit his sister. He had to stay in his room all morning.

pupil **Pupil** is another word for STUDENT.

puppy A **puppy** is a young dog.

purple **Purple** is a color that is part red and part blue.

purpose A **purpose** is a reason why a thing is made or done. The **purpose** of a coat is to keep you warm. If you mean to do a thing, you do it **on purpose.**

push To **push** is to use your hands to move something away. Jill **pushed** the door open.

put When you make a thing be in a certain place, you **put** it there. Mike **put** his coat in the closet. **Put** a period at the end of a sentence when you write. **—puts, put, putting.**

punctuation "The rain was heavy Matt ran under a tree but I didn't" You can probably guess what that means, but it's hard to read. The reason is that it has no **punctuation.** Now try it this way: "The rain was heavy. Matt ran under a tree, but I didn't." **Punctuation** is the name for the marks we put in a sentence to make it easier to understand, such as periods (.) and commas (,). Punctuation marks are like road signs. They tell you when to stop or slow down as you read.

Qq

a b c d e f g h i j k l m n o p q r s t u v w x y z

quart A **quart** is an amount of a liquid. There are 32 ounces in a **quart** and four **quarts** in a **gallon.**

quarter A **quarter** is a metal coin. One **quarter** is worth twenty-five cents.

queen A **queen** is a woman who rules a country. The wife of a king is also called a **queen.**

question When you want to find out about something, you ask a **question.** Teachers often ask **questions** to find out what their students know.

quick Something is **quick** if it is fast. Mom just took a **quick** trip to the store to get some bread.

quiet **Quiet** means not loud. Something **quiet** makes little or no noise. The girls were **quiet** as they listened to the music.

quit To **quit** is to stop doing something. Mr. Day wants to **quit** his job and get a new job.

quite Mark wasn't **quite** sure which bus to take home. Kate wasn't **quite** ready when we came to pick her up.

questions **Questions** are sentences that ask <u>for</u> something or ask <u>about</u> something. A question ends with a **question mark** (**?**) Here are some questions: "Is that your dog**?**" "What time is it**?**"

There are two kinds of questions. A **yes/no question** is one like "Is that your dog?" The answer to a question like this is always either "yes" or "no." The other kind of question is an **information question,** such as "What time is it?" or "Who wrote that book?". This kind asks for some kind of information as an answer, not just "yes" or "no."

93

R r

a b c d e f g h i j k l m n o p q r s t u v w x y z

rabbit A **rabbit** is an animal. A **rabbit** is about as big as a cat. **Rabbits** have soft fur, big front teeth, long ears, and a short tail.

race A **race** is a contest to see who or what is the fastest. The girls in our class had a **race** across the playground.

radio A **radio** is a thing you can listen to. **Radio** stations send sounds out in the air. Miyako listens to music on her **radio**.

railroad A **railroad** is a path for trains. A **railroad** has long metal **tracks** that the train's wheels go on. A company that runs trains is also called a **railroad.**

rain **Rain** is water that falls in drops from the sky. **Rain** helps plants to grow. Do you think it will **rain** today?

raise **1.** To **raise** something is to lift it up or move it to a higher place. Jo **raised** the window to let in some fresh air. **Raise** your hand if you know the answer. **2.** To **raise** also means to help a thing grow. My Dad **raises** beans in his garden. Heather has **raised** those cats since they were kittens.

ran Ella **ran** down the street to catch the bus. **Ran** is a form of the word RUN.

rather I'd **rather** have pizza than chicken for dinner tonight. Kelly loves to read. She'd **rather** read than watch television.

reach To **reach** is to put out your hand to try to hold or touch something. Tony **reached** up to catch the ball.
—**reaches, reached, reaching.**

94

read To **read** is to look at words and know what they mean. Peg likes to **read** books about horses. Last week she **read** a book that was called "Black Beauty." —**reads, read, reading.**

ready To be **ready** means you have everything you need to do something. Tina got her books and put on her coat, so she was **ready** to go to school.

real When a thing is **real,** it is true. My friends call me Chip, but my **real** name is Walter. Are those flowers **real** or plastic?

really 1. **Really** means actually or in a real way. Did Mom **really** say we could have soda instead of milk with dinner? 2. **Really** also means very. The winters here are **really** cold.

reason A **reason** tells you why something has happened. The **reason** so few trees grow here is that it doesn't rain enough.

recess **Recess** is a time at school when students stop class and go outside to play.

rectangle A **rectangle** is a shape. It has four straight sides. The front of a book has the shape of a **rectangle**.

red **Red** is a bright color. Blood is **red.** The American flag has **red** and white stripes.

refrigerator A **refrigerator** is a large machine that keeps food cold and fresh.

regular Something **regular** is like most other things of its kind. Noon is the **regular** time to have lunch. "Walk" is a **regular verb.** (See the box on page 51.)

relative A **relative** is a person in the same family. Your parents, grandparents, brothers, sisters, aunts, uncles, and cousins are your **relatives.** A person who is your **relative** is **related** to you.

red "She owns a <u>car</u>. He owns a <u>truck</u>." A truck and a car are two different things. "She owns a **red** <u>car</u>. He owns a **blue** <u>car</u>." Here, the two things are the same. Both are cars. But the words <u>red</u> and <u>blue</u> tell us that they are different. <u>Car</u> and <u>truck</u> are **nouns.** They <u>name</u> things. <u>Red</u> and <u>blue</u> are describing words, or **adjectives.** (Say it as ADD-juh-tiv.) An adjective tells something more about a noun. It shows how one thing is different from other things of the same kind. An <u>old</u> truck is not the same as a <u>new</u> truck. <u>New</u> and <u>old</u> are adjectives.

rhyme   If two words end with the same sound, they **rhyme.** For example, the word <u>rhyme</u> sounds like <u>time</u>.

      Up came the <u>sun</u>   It was a soft <u>night</u>
      She started to <u>run</u>.   Warm without <u>light</u>.
      The words <u>sun</u> and <u>run</u> rhyme. The words <u>night</u> and <u>light</u> rhyme.
Words that rhyme are often used in songs and poems. They make a song or poem fun to hear and say. What rhyming words do you know?

relax   To **relax** is to take it easy without work or worry. Jane's favorite way to **relax** is to go to the beach and play in the sand.

remember   To **remember** a thing means to think of it again or keep it in mind. **Remember** to turn off the lights when you leave. I've met him before, but I can't **remember** his name.

repeat   To **repeat** something is to do it again. I didn't hear you. Please **repeat** what you said.

report   A **report** tells the facts about something. The weather **report** says that it may rain today. We have to write a book **report** about a book we've read.

rest   1. A **rest** is when you sleep or relax for a short time. I'm tired. I need to lie down and **rest** for a while.
2. **The rest** is what is left over. I kept one part of the newspaper and threw **the rest** away.

restaurant   A **restaurant** is a place you can go to buy a meal. In **restaurants,** people cook your food and bring it to you.

return   To **return** is to come back or go back. Birds fly south in the winter and **return** in the spring. Mary **returned** her library book.

rhyme   Words that **rhyme** end with the same sound. The words "cat" and "hat" **rhyme.** (See the box on this page.)

rice   Rice is a food. It comes from a kind of grass plant. People eat **rice** in many parts of the world.

rich   Rich people have a lot of money and other things. Someone who has a million dollars is very **rich.**

ride   To **ride** is to sit on or in something that moves. Elena likes to **ride** horses. I went for a **ride** in my uncle's new car.
—rides, rode, ridden, riding.

right **1.** Things have a **right** side and a LEFT side. Cars drive on the **right** side of the road.
2. When a thing is **right,** it is not wrong. Ten is the **right** answer to "how much is six and four?"

ring **1.** To **ring** is to make a certain sound. Did you hear the phone **ring** just now?
2. A **ring** is also a shape. It is a circle that is open in the middle. **Rings** are pieces of jewelry with this shape. You wear a **ring** on your finger.

rise To **rise** is to go up. Smoke **rises** from a fire. The sun **rose** at 6:30 this morning.
—**rises, rose, rising.**

river A **river** is a place where water moves through the land. The Amazon **River** is one of the longest **rivers** in the world.

The Amazon **River** is in South America.

road A **road** is a smooth, wide path made for cars and trucks to go on. Cars drive on the right side of the **road.**

rob To **rob** is to take someone's money or other things in a way that is against the law.
—**robs, robbed, robbing.**

rock **1.** A **rock** is a very hard thing that is found on or in the ground.
2. To **rock** means to move from side to side. The mother **rocked** the baby in her arms until he stopped crying.

roll **1.** To **roll** means to turn over many times. The ball **rolled** down the hill.
2. A **roll** is anything rolled up into a round shape. Erin bought two **rolls** of film for her camera.
3. A **roll** is a small, round kind of bread.

roof A **roof** is the top cover of a building. The rain sounded loud as it fell on the **roof.**

room A **room** is a place inside a building. Houses have **rooms** where people do different things. My family watches TV in our **living room**. We eat dinner in the **dining room.**

rope A **rope** is a thick and heavy kind of string. We used the **rope** to climb up the tree.

rose A **rose** is a kind of flower. **Roses** smell sweet and come in many different colors.

Roses can be red, pink, yellow, or white.

rough A thing that feels **rough** is not smooth. The rocks at the beach were **rough,** and it hurt my feet to walk on them. We drove the car slowly down the **rough** road.

round A **round** thing has the shape of a ball or a circle. An orange is a **round** fruit. Tires and rings are **round.**

row When things are in a **row,** they are in a straight line. A farmer plants corn in **rows**. At the game we sat in the first **row** of seats, right by the field.

rub When you **rub** something, you touch it and move your hand around on it. Mom **rubbed** Kim's back to help her get to sleep.

rude When people are **rude,** they are not being polite. It's **rude** to talk while the teacher is saying something to the class.

rug A **rug** is a thing that covers a floor. It is also called a **carpet.**

rule A **rule** is something that tells you how to act. Mom has a **rule** that we must finish dinner before we get dessert. Running in the hall is against the **rules.**

run 1. To **run** is to go along by moving your legs very fast. Sue had to **run** to catch the ball. 2. To **run** also means to go. The car **ran** better after we fixed it. Water **runs** through this pipe. —**runs, ran, running.**

rush To **rush** means to hurry. As soon as school let out, Brandon **rushed** home to feed his dog.

S s

sad If you are **sad,** you feel bad. You are not happy. Tim was **sad** when he broke his favorite toy.

safe **Safe** means not in danger. To be **safe** when you cross the street, always look both ways.

said **Said** is a form of the word SAY. I asked her how old she was. She **said** she was seven.

sail A **sail** is a piece of heavy cloth that is tied to a boat. Wind pushes against the **sails** and makes the boat move. Going in a **sailboat** is called **sailing.**

salad **Salad** is something to eat. Most **salads** are eaten cold and are made of vegetables or fruit.

sale A **sale** is when you can buy things for a lower price. The clothing store had a big **sale.**

salt **Salt** is something that is put on food to make it taste better.

same **1.** If two things are alike, they are the **same.** Six and 6 are ways to write the **same** number. **2.** If one thing does not change, it stays the **same.** I have lived in the **same** house all my life.

sand **Sand** is made up of very tiny pieces of rock. It is found on beaches and in deserts.

sandwich A **sandwich** is a thing to eat. **Sandwiches** have two pieces of bread with other food put between them.

sang The children **sang** three songs in the school play. **Sang** is a form of the word SING.

sat I **sat** and waited for the bus. **Sat** is a form of the word SIT.

Saturday   The word Saturday is called a **proper noun** or **proper name.** Proper here means "special" or "one of a kind." Proper names are a kind of noun, but they are different from other nouns. They name only one thing. There are different days, but only one called Saturday. There are many cities, but only one called Detroit. George Jones is the name of one certain person. Day, city, and person are called **common nouns.** Saturday, Detroit, and George Jones are proper names. Notice that a proper name begins with a capital letter: **D**etroit, not detroit.

Saturday   **Saturday** is a day of the week. **Saturday** comes after Friday and before Sunday.

save   **1.** If you **save** something, you keep it to use later. Keisha is **saving** her money to buy a new bike.
2. To **save** also means to keep someone from being hurt. The police officer **saved** a man from being run over by a bus.

saw   **Saw** is a form of the word SEE. I **saw** the movie "The Snow Goose" on TV last night.

saw   A **saw** is a tool used to cut wood and other things.

say   To **say** means to speak words out loud. What did the teacher **say**? I didn't hear what she **said.** —**says, said, saying.**

scare   To **scare** means to make afraid. The loud noise **scared** the baby, and he started to cry.

school   A **school** is a place where you go to learn things. You learn to read in **school**.

science   **Science** is everything that people know or try to know about nature, the earth, and space. A person who works in **science** is called a **scientist.**

scissors   **Scissors** are used to cut things. A pair of **scissors** has two sharp pieces of metal that close against each other.

score   To **score** means to make a point in a game. The Bears just **scored**. The **score** is now 6 to 4.

scratch   To **scratch** is to cut or dig with something sharp. Andrea **scratched** her arm on the rose bush.

scream   A **scream** is a loud cry. People **scream** when they are hurt or afraid. Kelly **screamed** when she saw the big spider.

screen   **1.** A **screen** is a thing put on a window or door to keep out insects. **Screens** are metal and have tiny holes to let air in. **2.** The part of a television set that you watch is called a **screen.**

sea   A **sea** is a large area of salt water like an ocean. A **sea** is not as big as an ocean.

This town is on the Mediterranean **Sea.**

season   A **season** is a certain time of the year. The four **seasons** are spring, summer, fall, and winter.

seat   A **seat** is a place where you can sit. A chair is a kind of **seat.**

second   **1. Second** comes right after first. Carol was the **second** person in line, behind Rose. **2.** A **second** is a short amount of time. There are sixty **seconds** in one minute.

secret   A **secret** is something that you know but don't tell about. We kept Dad's surprise party a **secret** until his birthday.

see   To **see** means to look at things with your eyes. Cats **see** in the dark better than we do. Please move out of the way. I can't **see** the TV.
—**sees, saw, seen, seeing.**

seem   **Seem** means to look or be like. Is Tommy really only six? He **seems** much older than that.

seen   Have you **seen** that movie? **Seen** is a form of the word SEE.

selfish   Someone who is **selfish** thinks only of himself. It was **selfish** of Jackie to take all the apples and not give any to us.

sell   To **sell** a thing is to turn it over to someone who gives you money for it. He wants to **sell** his old car and buy a new one. That store **sells** all kinds of toys.

send   To **send** something is to make it go from one place to another. Anita **sends** a birthday card to her grandmother every year. Mom **sent** my brother to the store to buy some milk.
—**sends, sent, sending.**

sentences When we write, we put words together. Here is a group of words: "dog the away." Those are easy words. You know what each of them means by itself. But what do they mean together? Nothing. What about these words? "The dog ran away." Now you <u>do</u> have a meaning. "**The dog ran away.**" is a **sentence.** A sentence has to be in the right order ("dog the away" is not right). It has to have both a noun (such as <u>dog</u>) and a verb (such as <u>ran</u>). It has to tell an idea all by itself. Also, in writing it has to begin with a capital letter and end with a period.

sentence A **sentence** is a group of words that tells a complete thought. "Bill and Tony" is <u>not</u> a **sentence.** "Bill and Tony went home" <u>is</u> a **sentence.** It tells what happened, and who did it.

serious 1. If you're **serious,** you're not making a joke. Are you **serious?** Did you really win the spelling contest?
2. If a problem is **serious,** it is important or dangerous. He has to stay in the hospital because he has a **serious** illness.

serve To **serve** food means to put it out for people to eat. That restaurant **serves** lunch and dinner every day of the week.

set 1. To **set** is to put a thing in a certain place. When you **set** the table, you put the dishes, knives, and forks in a certain place.
2. A **set** is a group of things that belong together. Charlie got a **set** of toy trains for his birthday.

seven **Seven** is the word for the number **7**. **Seven** comes after six and before eight.

several **Several** means more than two, but not many. This coat comes in **several** colors—blue, gray, black, and brown.

shadow A **shadow** is a dark area. **Shadows** are caused by something in the way of the sunlight. If the sun shines on the left side of a tree, you'll see the tree's **shadow** on the right.

shake To **shake** means to move quickly up and down or from side to side. On the medicine bottle it said, "**Shake** well before using." The men **shook** hands when they met on the street. **—shakes, shook, shaken, shaking.**

shape The **shape** of a thing is its outside form. Circles, squares, and triangles are **shapes.**

share To **share** a thing is to let someone else use it or have part of it. Steven **shared** his lunch with his little brother.

sharp Something that is **sharp** has an edge or a point that can cut easily. Michelle used a **sharp** knife to cut up the apple.

she **She** is a word used to talk about a girl or woman. Mom said **she** has to go to the store.

sheep A **sheep** is a farm animal. **Sheep** are raised for food and for their thick curly hair, which is called **wool.** Wool is used to make clothing.

This **sheep** has a thick coat of wool.

shell A **shell** is the hard outside part that covers and guards the body of certain animals such as the turtle. Eggs, nuts, and seeds also have **shells.**

shine 1. To **shine** means to give off light. The sky was blue, and the sun was **shining** brightly. 2. To **shine** a thing is to make it bright. Paul **shined** his shoes.

ship A **ship** is a very big boat. **Ships** carry people and things across the ocean.

shirt A **shirt** is a thing to wear. You wear a **shirt** on the top part of your body. Boys and men wear **shirts.**

shoe A **shoe** is something you wear on your foot.

shook **Shook** is a form of the word SHAKE.

shoot 1. To **shoot** means to fire a gun. The hunter **shot** at a deer. 2. To **shoot** also means to try to get a goal in basketball or soccer. **—shoots, shot, shooting.**

shop A **shop** is a place that sells things. A store that sells meat is called a **butcher shop.** To **shop** is to go to **shops** to buy things. Kim went **shopping** for a new jacket.

shore The **shore** is the land at the edge of an ocean, lake, or river. We stepped out of the boat and on to the **shore.**

showing   Let's say that you're walking in the woods and you see an unusual old house. You want to tell your Mom about it. If you have a camera, you can take a picture that will **show** her just what it looks like.

You can also use words to "show" what the house looks like. Try to paint a picture with your words. Don't just write, "It was a strange old house. I was scared." **Show** your reader the house: "Grass and bushes grew right up to the front door. The windows were painted black. There was no front door, just a space where the door had been."

short   **Short** means not tall or long. Lee just got a haircut, and his hair is really **short** now. She is the **shortest** girl in her class. Ten seconds is a **short** time.

shot   **1. Shot** is a form of the word SHOOT. The soccer player took a **shot** at the goal. **2.** A **shot** is medicine that a doctor or nurse puts into your body with a special point.

should   If you are supposed to do something, you **should** do it. You **should** look both ways before you cross the street.

shoulder   A **shoulder** is part of your body. Your **shoulders** are between your neck and arms.

shout   To **shout** means to cry out loudly. "Hey! Watch where you're going!" the man **shouted** when I almost hit him with my bike.
—**shouts, shouted, shouting.**

show   **1.** To **show** something is to let it be seen. Robbie **showed** his new bike to his friends. (See the box on this page.) **2.** A **show** is a story on TV, in a play, or at the movies. "Sesame Street" is my favorite TV **show**.

shut   To **shut** something is to close it. Billy went in the house and **shut** the door behind him.

shy   A **shy** person feels quiet and a little afraid around other people. Alice doesn't say much in class, because she's too **shy**.

sick   When you are **sick**, you don't feel well. Doctors and nurses take care of **sick** people.

side   **1.** A **side** is part of a thing. The doors of a car are on the **sides**. A square has four **sides**. A piece of paper has two **sides**. **2.** A **side** is one of two teams in a game or contest. Let's choose up **sides** and play baseball.

sight Sight is how or what you see. The dog ran out of **sight** around the corner. People wear glasses to help their **eyesight.**

sign 1. A **sign** is a board with words or marks on it to tell people something. Stop **signs** on the road tell drivers to stop. 2. A **sign** is a mark or object that stands for something. The + **sign** means that you should add two numbers together. 3. To **sign** means to write your name. **Sign** your name on the back of your new library card.

The **sign** tells drivers not to go ahead.

signal A **signal** is something that gives a warning or message. The flashing **signal** told us that a train was coming.

silence Silence is when there is no sound. Something **silent** makes no sound. The letter k̲ in the word k̲not is **silent.**

silly 1. Something that is **silly** is funny. The people laughed at the **silly** things the clown did. 2. **Silly** can also mean not using good thinking. I made a **silly** mistake on the spelling test.

silver Silver is a kind of metal that is worth a lot of money. It has a shiny white color. **Silver** is used in jewelry, coins, and other things. Knives, forks, and spoons are called **silverware.**

similar Two things that are like each other are **similar**. A wolf looks **similar** to a large dog.

simple Something that is easy to do is **simple**. 1 + 1 = 2 is a **simple** arithmetic problem.

since 1. Since means from then until now. She moved away last year. I haven't seen her **since.** 2. **Since** also means because. Few plants grow in a desert, **since** there's so little rain there.

sing To **sing** is to make music with the voice. You **sing** a song. —**sings, sang, sung, singing.**

single Single means only one. All the students lined up in a **single** line. A person who is not married is said to be **single.**

105

sleeping, sitting, skating   The words <u>sleep</u>, <u>sit</u>, and <u>skate</u> are verbs. The letters **ing** go at the end of a verb to show a different use of the word. "Danny likes to <u>sleep</u> late on weekends. It's 10:00 and he's still <u>sleeping</u>." "Do you mind if I <u>sit</u> in this chair? Is anyone <u>sitting</u> here?" "Lisa just learned to ice <u>skate</u>. She goes <u>skating</u> all the time now."
        Please note the way **ing** is added to <u>sit</u> and <u>skate</u>. <u>Sit</u> doubles the letter at the end to make <u>sitting</u>. <u>Skate</u> drops the **e** at the end, <u>skating</u>.

sink   **1.** A **sink** is a place used for washing things. He washed the dishes in the kitchen **sink**.
2. To **sink** means to go down below the water. Our old boat **sank** in the lake. By the time we got there, it had already **sunk** to the bottom.
—**sinks, sank, sunk, sinking.**

sister   Your **sister** is a girl or woman who has the same mother and father that you have.

sit   To **sit** means to rest on the lower part of your back. Dad always **sits** in his favorite chair when he watches TV.
—**sits, sat, sitting.**

six   **Six** is the word for the number **6**. **Six** comes after five and before seven.

size   The **size** of a thing is how big or little it is. Elephants are known for their very large **size**. She wears a **size** 6 shoe.

skate   A **skate** is a special kind of shoe. **Roller skates** have four wheels on the bottom and are used to move on sidewalks or other hard surfaces. **Ice skates** have a long piece of metal on the bottom and are used on ice.

skin   Your **skin** is the thin covering on the outside of your body. If you play in the sun all day, your **skin** can get burned.

sky   The **sky** is the area that is above the earth. At night we look at stars in the **sky**. Today the sun is shining, and the **skies** are blue.

sleep   To **sleep** is to rest with your eyes closed. Most people **sleep** at night. When you **sleep**, you don't see or hear things around you. I **slept** late today.
—**sleeps, slept, sleeping.**

sleeve   The **sleeves** are the parts of a piece of clothing that cover your arms.

slide To **slide** is to move across something in a smooth, easy way. Jennifer took a run and **slid** across the ice. A **slide** is a toy on a playground. It has a long, smooth part that you **slide** down. —**slides, slid, sliding.**

slip To **slip** means to slide or move suddenly. Greg **slipped** and fell on the ice.

slow A thing that is **slow** is not fast. A snail is a **slow**-moving animal. The bus driver drove **slowly** up to the bus stop.

small Something that is **small** is not big. It is little. A baby is very **small.** We live in a **small** town.

smart **Smart** people can use their minds well. They know things and are good at thinking. My sister is so **smart** that she taught herself to read before she went to school.

smell To **smell** means to know something by using your nose. When Ramon **smelled** smoke, he called the Fire Department. These flowers have a nice **smell.**

smile People **smile** when they feel happy. Tracy **smiled** when she saw her best friend walk in.

smoke **Smoke** goes up from a fire. It looks like a white, gray, or black cloud. The **smoke** from the campfire made Erin cough. —**smokes, smoked, smoking.**

smooth Something that is not rough is **smooth.** Babies have **smooth** skin. The airplane made a **smooth** landing.

snack A **snack** is a little bit of food that you eat between meals. Robin always has a **snack** when she gets home from school.

snake A **snake** is an animal. A **snake** has a long thin body with no arms or legs. **Snakes** move by sliding along the ground. Some **snakes** have poison in their bite, but most do not.

This **snake** is known as the "king cobra" because it is so large. It is very poisonous.

snow   **Snow** is a kind of soft, frozen rain. **Snow** falls from clouds to the ground in little white pieces called **snowflakes**.

snow   This **snowflake** is caught on a leaf.

so   **1. So** means very much. I'm **so** glad you're coming with us! **2. So** means also or in the same way. Gil likes cake, and **so** do I. **3. So** also means because of that. Chrissie missed the bus, **so** she had to walk home.

soap   **Soap** is something used to clean other things. We wash our hands with a bar of **soap.**

soccer   **Soccer** is a game played on a field by two teams. Each team tries to kick the ball into the other team's goal.

sock   A **sock** is something you wear on your foot. You wear your shoes over your **socks.**

soda   A **soda** is a sweet drink. **Soda** has tiny air bubbles in it.

soft   **1. Soft** means not hard or rough. Kittens have **soft** fur. **2. Soft** also means not too strong. **Soft** lights are not bright. She sang to the baby in a **soft** voice.

sold   **Sold** is a form of the word SELL. Our neighbors **sold** their house and moved away.

soldier   A person in the army is a **soldier. Soldiers** fight in wars.

solid   **1.** A thing that is **solid** is not a liquid or a gas. Ice is the **solid** form of water. **2. Solid** also means all one color or kind. This ring is **solid** gold.

some   Do you have **some** paper I could use? I've read **some** of that book, but not all of it.

somebody   **Somebody** means a person. **Somebody** left this note for you. **Someone** means the same thing as **somebody**.

something   **Something** means a thing. I need **something** to eat.

sometimes   **Sometimes** means now and then. Most days are dry here, but **sometimes** it rains.

somewhere Somewhere means in or to some place. I know I left my book **somewhere** around here, but I can't find it. **Someplace** means the same thing as **somewhere.**

son A boy or man is the **son** of his mother and father. They have two **sons** and a daughter.

song A **song** is music that you sing. "White Christmas" is a famous **song.** The robin is a bird that has a pretty **song.**

soon Soon means in a short time. Beth called to say she'd be here **soon.** Our dog ran off, but he came back **soon** after.

sore When something is **sore**, it hurts. Ed's leg is **sore** where he got kicked in the soccer game.

sorry If you are **sorry**, you feel sad. Toni was **sorry** that she lost her friend's doll. I'm **sorry** to hear that your mother is sick.

sound A **sound** is anything that you can hear. I love to hear the **sound** of the waves at the beach.

soup Soup is something to eat. **Soup** is made by cooking meat, fish, or vegetables in water or some other liquid.

sour Sour things have a sharp, biting taste. Lemons are **sour**.

south South is a direction on the earth. When you look at the sunset, **south** is on your left.

space 1. **Space** is the name for all the area beyond the earth's air. The sun, moon, planets, and stars are all in **space**.
2. A **space** is an empty area between things. We put a **space** between words when we write.

speak To **speak** is to talk. In Mexico people **speak** Spanish. (See the box on this page.) —**speaks, spoke, spoken, speaking.**

speaking and writing The two different ways that we use words are when we <u>speak</u> and when we <u>write</u>. Either way, we have to put the words together to make <u>sentences</u>.

There are some important differences between writing and speaking. You have to be more careful when you write, and watch for mistakes. You can't stop yourself and say something over, the way you can when you talk. And you can't stop between words to show a new idea. You have to show this with a comma, or with a period.

special A **special** thing is different from other things. Today's my birthday. Mom is fixing a **special** meal for me.

speech A **speech** is a talk that a person gives to a group. The President made a **speech** to a group of business leaders.

spell To **spell** a word is to put its letters in the right order. "Cat" is **spelled** C-A-T. Putting letters together in this way is **spelling**. (See the box on this page.)

spend To **spend** is to pay money for something. Tommy **spent** all his money on that new toy. —**spends, spent, spending.**

spider A **spider** is a very small animal. **Spiders** have eight legs and no wings. **Spiders** make **webs** to catch insects for food.

spill To **spill** is to let or make something fall out. Bill **spilled** a glass of milk all over the table.

spoon A **spoon** is a thing you eat with. A **spoon** has a handle. It has a round part on one end.

spoke Our teacher **spoke** to us about the school science fair. Mom has **spoken** to me several times about not leaving papers on the floor. **Spoke** and **spoken** are forms of the word SPEAK.

sport A **sport** is a game. Soccer, baseball, and swimming are my favorite **sports**.

spot A **spot** is a small mark. While he was painting, Ted got **spots** of paint on his shirt. Our dog is white with black **spots**.

spread 1. To **spread** is to open wide. The bird **spread** its wings. 2. **Spread** also means to cover with something. I **spread** some butter on a piece of bread.

spring **Spring** is a season of the year. **Spring** comes after winter and before summer.

spelling The letters we use to write a word are the **spelling** of the word. A word can be spelled right or wrong. Suppose someone left you a note that said, "Give the car some milk." Give the <u>car</u> some milk? It should have said "cat." It's important to spell words the right way.

Some words, such as <u>sit</u> and <u>step</u>, aren't too hard to spell. You can tell from the sound how they should be spelled. But many other words do not sound the way they are spelled, such as <u>square</u>, <u>stage</u>, <u>stairs</u>, <u>station</u>, and <u>steal</u>. That is why people use dictionaries!

square A **square** is a shape with four sides. All four sides of a **square** are the same size.

squirrel A **squirrel** is a small animal with a long tail and red, gray, or dark brown fur. Most **squirrels** live in trees.

squirrel This is the gray **squirrel.**

stage A **stage** is the high place at the front of a theater where the actors stand to put on a play.

stairs A **stair** is a step. **Stairs** are a group of steps. You go **upstairs** to the second floor of a house.

stamp A **stamp** is a small piece of paper showing that you paid to mail a letter.

stand When you are **standing**, you are up on your feet. I **stood** in line to get into the movie.
—**stands, stood, standing.**

star 1. A **star** looks like a bright spot of light in the sky. **Stars** are actually huge balls of fire that are far, far away in space.
2. A person who has the main part in a movie is called a **star.**

start To **start** means to begin or get going. School **starts** at 8:00. He **started** the car and drove off.

state A **state** is one of the fifty parts of the **United States.** Dallas is a city in the **state** of Texas.

station A **station** is a place where special things are done. Trains go out from a **railroad station.** Police officers work at a **police station**.

stay To **stay** is to be in the same place for a time. Ricardo had to **stay** home from school today because he was sick.

steal To **steal** is to take things in a way that is against the law. The police are after a man who **stole** money from the bank.

step You **step** when you lift your foot and put it down in another place. He **stepped** back to let me get by. A **step** is a place to put your foot. Stairs have **steps.**
—**stepped, stepping.**

story writing Are all **stories** make-believe? No. Many stories are true to life. A **history** of the United States tells the story of America's past. A **biography** of a famous person like Benjamin Franklin tells that person's life story. Even when you make up a story, it can be like real life. You don't have to write about strange beings from space or animals that talk. You can get ideas from real people and real things. Whatever kind of story you write, it should have a good beginning, middle, and end.

stick **1.** A **stick** is a long, thin piece of wood.
2. To **stick** means to be held or caught in one place. The car's wheels were **stuck** in the mud.

still **1. Still** means not moving. Dad told me to sit **still** while he cut my hair.
2. Still means just as before. Do you **still** live on Oak Street?

stomach Your **stomach** is part of your body. After you eat food, it goes to your **stomach**.

stone A **stone** is a small piece of rock. The boys were throwing **stones** into the lake.

stop To **stop** is to not move or go on. When the **stop** light turned red, she **stopped** her car. **Stop** playing with your food and eat.

store A **store** is a place that sells things. John went to the **store** to buy some milk. The shoe **store** is having a sale this week.

storm A **storm** is a change in the weather that brings strong winds along with rain or snow.

story A **story** tells about a thing that happened. There was a **story** in the paper about a fire. "Rip Van Winkle" is the **story** of a man who slept for 20 years.

stove A **stove** is a thing we use for cooking food. Tina cooked some eggs on top of the **stove.**

straight If a line is **straight,** it does not curve or go off to the side. It goes like this. —————

strange Something **strange** is very different or unusual. Lisa heard **strange** noises outside in the dark and got really worried.

street A **street** is a road in a city or town. It has houses or other buildings on one or both sides.

string **String** is long and thin. It is used to tie or hold things.

stripe   **Stripes** are lines of color. The American flag has red and white **stripes.**

strong   Something that is **strong** has a lot of power. **Strong** people can lift heavy things. A **strong** wind blew over the tree.

student   A **student** is a person who goes to school. Mrs. Long has 25 **students** in her class.

study   To **study** something is to learn about it by reading and thinking. Tom **studied** hard for the math test.

subject   A **subject** is something you study in school. Reading, spelling, and math are **subjects.**

subtract   To **subtract** means to take one number away from another. If you **subtract** three from four, you get one. Doing this is called **subtraction.**

such   **Such** means "so much so." It was **such** a cold day that we stayed inside all day.

sudden   Something **sudden** happens very quickly and is not expected. The driver made a **sudden** stop. **Suddenly** the sky got dark and it started to rain.

sugar   **Sugar** is something we use to make foods sweet. Juan put some **sugar** on his cereal.

suit   A **suit** is a set of clothes that are made to be worn together. Most **suits** have a skirt or pants and a matching jacket. Men who work in offices wear **suits.**

summer   **Summer** is a season of the year. **Summer** comes after spring and before fall.

sun   The **sun** is a star. The **sun** gives us light and heat. The earth moves around the **sun.** The **sun** comes up at **sunrise** and goes down at **sunset.** If it is a **sunny** day, there is plenty of **sunshine.**

Sunset over the Pacific Ocean.

Sunday **Sunday** is the first day of the week. **Sunday** comes after Saturday and before Monday.

supermarket A **supermarket** is a large store that sells food and things you use in your home.

suppose If you are **supposed** to do something, you are expected to do it. Jason was **supposed** to clean his room before he went out to play, but he didn't do it.

sure If you know you are right about a thing, you are **sure** of it. I'm **sure** that Paris is the capital of France. I just read it in a book.

surface The **surface** of a thing is its outside or top part. The rock had a rough **surface.** We could see the fish swimming just below the **surface** of the water.

surprise You are **surprised** when something happens that you didn't expect. Joan's friends had a **surprise** party for her on her birthday. They **surprised** her with cake and presents.

sweater A **sweater** is a thing you wear to keep warm. You can wear it over a shirt. Many **sweaters** are made of wool.

sweet Something that is **sweet** tastes like sugar. Fruit, candy, and ice cream are **sweet.**

swim You **swim** when you use your arms and legs to move along or stay up in the water. This is called **swimming.** A person who does this is a **swimmer.**
—**swims, swam, swum, swimming.**

swing To **swing** is to move through the air in a curve or circle. The children were **swinging** from a rope on a tree. Mario **swung** his bat and hit the baseball. A **swing** is a seat you can **swing** on.
—**swings, swung, swinging.**

system A system is a way to do things or put things together. All the schools in a town make up the town's school **system.**

synonyms If you are <u>sure</u> that something is true, you are <u>certain</u> about it. "I'm <u>sure</u> the door is locked. I'm <u>certain</u> I locked it." <u>Certain</u> and <u>sure</u> mean the same thing. When two words mean the same thing, they are called **synonyms.** The word **synonym** actually means "same name." If a word is the opposite of another word, it is an **antonym.** Hot-cold or happy-sad are antonyms. The word **antonym** means "opposite name."

T t

a b c d e f g h i j k l m n o p q r s t u v w x y z

table   A **table** is a piece of furniture. **Tables** have a flat top and four legs. The family sat at the kitchen **table** to eat dinner.

tail   The part of an animal's body that sticks out from the back is its **tail.** A monkey uses its **tail** to swing from trees.

take   If you **take** something, you get it or have it. Mom **takes** my hand when we cross the street. **Take** this box out to the garage. Dad **took** us to the park today.
—**takes, took, taken, taking.**

tale   A **tale** is a make-believe story. **Tales** like "Snow White" are also called **fairy tales.**

talk   To **talk** is to say words. The baby is learning to **talk.** Mom is **talking** to Dad on the telephone.
—**talks, talked, talking.**

tall   Something **tall** is not short. It is high off the ground. A giraffe is a very **tall** animal. New York City has lots of **tall** buildings.

taste   When you **taste** food, you put it in your mouth and find out what it's like. Lemons **taste** sour. This soup **tastes** great!

teach   To **teach** is to help a person know about something. I **taught** my little brother how to count to ten. Dad is **teaching** me to swim.
—**teaches, taught, teaching.**

teacher   A **teacher** is a person who teaches in a school or gives lessons.

team   In sports, a **team** is a group of people who play together. There are nine players on a baseball **team.**

tear To **tear** a thing is to pull it into pieces. Bob didn't like what he'd written. He decided to **tear** up his paper and start over. This word sounds like "air." —**tears, tore, tearing.**

tear A **tear** is a drop of water that runs down from your eye when you cry. This word sounds like "deer."

teenager A **teenager** is a person who is between thirteen and nineteen years old.

teeth **Teeth** means "more than one tooth." You should brush your **teeth** after meals.

telephone A **telephone** is used for talking to someone. When you speak into a **telephone**, the sound moves through a wire to the person you are calling.

telescope A **telescope** makes things that are very far away seem to be closer and larger. **Telescopes** are used to look at the stars and planets.

television A **television** shows pictures and sound. People watch **television** at home. **Television** stations send sounds and pictures out in the air.

tell To **tell** something is to let people know about it. I have to **tell** Mrs. Lewis I won't be riding home with her today. Dad **told** me I have to clean my room. —**tells, told, telling.**

temperature The **temperature** of something is how hot or cold it is. Water turns to ice at a **temperature** of 32.

ten **Ten** is the word for the number **10**. **Ten** is one more than nine.

tennis **Tennis** is a game played by two or four players who hit a ball with a thing called a **racket.**

terrible Something **terrible** is very, very bad. I saw a **terrible** car accident on the road today. That was a **terrible** movie!

telescope This huge **telescope** is on top of a mountain in Southern California.

the Of all the words in English, which one do you think is used most often? You may have guessed it. The word used most often is the. Any time people talk or write about a certain thing, they use the word the—the house, the dog, the movies, the red car.

How do we know that the is the most common word? We used a computer to look through thousands of books, newspapers, and magazines. The computer "read" ten million words in all. It counted how often each word was used. The was used 650,000 times, nearly four times as often as the number 2 word, and.

test A **test** is a way to find out what you have learned. A **test** has questions to answer.

than 1. **Than** is used to show how two things are different from each other. A bear is much bigger **than** a dog.
2. **Than** is also used to show which of two things someone wants to do or have. I'd rather have chicken **than** fish.

thank To **thank** means to tell someone that you like what he or she did for you. Scott **thanked** me for helping him wash the dishes. **"Thank you,"** he said.

Thanksgiving **Thanksgiving** is a holiday in November. On **Thanksgiving**, we give thanks for all the good things we have.

that See **that** man over there? **That's** my Dad. It was so cold **that** I put on my winter coat.

the The is used to point out or name a certain person or thing. (See the box on this page.)

theater A **theater** is a place where people go to see movies or plays. There are two movie **theaters** at the shopping center.

their If two or more people have something, it is **their** thing. All the children put on **their** coats. The Wilsons planted a tree in **their** back yard. Our cat is black, but **theirs** is white.

them When a thing happens to people, it happens to **them.** My parents came to my school. I showed **them** my work.

then 1. **Then** means at that time. We used to live in New York, but I was just a baby **then.**
2. **Then** also means next. First put in the meat. **Then** put in the potatoes and **then** the vegetables.

> **there, their, they're**   Here are three words that are very much like each other. See if you can tell the difference. "**There** is the Millers' house. **Their** grandson Todd is in my class at school. **They're** very nice people." There is used to show where something is. Their means "of them" or "owned by them." They're is a short way to write "they are."
>   The way words are used is called **usage**. "Correct usage" means using words the right way, such as knowing when to use there or their or they're. If you're not sure which word to use, check your dictionary.

there   1. **There** means in, at, or to that place. Hawaii looks like a nice place. I'd like to go **there**. 2. **There are** is used to say that a thing is true. **There are** seven days in a week. (See the box on this page.)

thermometer   A **thermometer** tells how hot or cold the air is.

these   Those plants over there aren't growing well, but **these** plants are doing fine.

they   Paul and Sandy couldn't come with us. **They** had to stay home. **They're** is a short way to say or write "they are." **They're** sorry they couldn't come.

thick   **Thick** means big around. In old times castles were built with **thick** stone walls.

thin   **Thin** means not very big around. Ted wants a **thin** piece of cheese on his sandwich.

thing   **Things** are what you can see or think about. She acts as if her doll were a real baby, not just a **thing**. It's time for dinner. Take your **things** off the table.

think   **Think** means to use your mind to make ideas. Josh had to **think** very hard to answer all the test questions.

third   The **third** is next after the second. David was **third** in line, right behind Ben and Katie.

thirsty   When you are **thirsty**, you feel a need for something to drink. May I please have a glass of water? I'm very **thirsty**.

this   See **this** blue rock? I found it in the yard. **This** tree right here is a lemon tree. That one behind it is an orange tree.

those   These books right here are mine. **Those** books over there are my sister's.

though **Though** means even if. I like our new house, **though** it isn't as big as our old one was.

thought 1. I **thought** I'd like the movie, but I didn't. **Thought** is a form of the word THINK. 2. A **thought** is something you think. When Anna woke up this morning, her first **thought** was that she was late for school.

three **Three** is the word for the number **3**. **Three** is one more than two and one less than four.

throat The **throat** is the front of the neck. Food goes down your **throat** to your stomach.

through 1. **Through** is from one part to another. Jill walked **through** the woods. A rock went **through** the window. 2. **Through** means finished. I can go out and play now. I'm **through** with my homework.

throw To **throw** means to send something through the air. Ed **threw** the baseball to Larry. —**throws, threw, thrown, throwing.**

thumb Your **thumb** is the short, thick finger at the end of your hand.

thunder **Thunder** is a loud crashing sound that comes in a storm after a flash of lightning.

Thursday **Thursday** is a day of the week. **Thursday** comes after Wednesday and before Friday.

ticket A **ticket** is a piece of paper. People buy **tickets** to get into a movie or a game, to ride on a plane or train, and so on.

tie To **tie** things is to hold them with rope or string. The man **tied** the horse to a tree so that it wouldn't run away. —**ties, tied, tying.**

tiger A **tiger** is a wild animal. **Tigers** live in the jungle. **Tigers** are big cats with orange-brown fur and black stripes.

The **tiger** is the largest of the cat family.

tight **Tight** means not loose. This sweater is too **tight** for me. Hold on **tight** and don't let go!

till **Till** means the same thing as UNTIL. Jim played outdoors **till** his mother called him in.

time **1. Time** is what clocks show. **Time** is measured in hours, days, weeks, and so on. Dinosaurs lived a long **time** ago. The **time** right now is 10:30. **2.** The number of **times** a thing happens is how often it happens. That's the third **time** today that he's called you.

tiny **Tiny** means very, very small. Some insects are so **tiny** that we almost can't see them.

tired When you feel **tired**, you have little energy and you want to rest. Nikki was **tired** after playing soccer for two hours.

title The name of a story, book, song, or movie is its **title.** (See the box on this page.)

to I'm going **to** the store. Would you like **to** come with me?. The store is open from 10 **to** 6. Please give this note **to** Mom.

today **Today** is the day that it is right now. There's no school **today**. **Today** is a holiday.

toe A **toe** is part of your foot. You have five **toes** on each foot.

together Things that are with each other are **together.** To make lemonade, you put lemon juice, water, and sugar **together.** Andrew, Philip, and Eddie played **together** all afternoon.

told **Told** is a form of the word TELL. Maria **told** Dad what she learned in school today.

tomato A **tomato** is a round, juicy fruit. **Tomatoes** are red.

tomorrow **Tomorrow** is the day after today. Today is Wednesday. **Tomorrow** will be Thursday.

---

titles The **title** of a story, book, or poem is its name. The name of that book is "Going Home." Its <u>title</u> is "Going Home." Here are some <u>titles</u>: "The Long Winter;" "Little House on the Prairie;" "Goodnight Moon."

 When you write a story or poem, write the title above the first line. Use a capital letter for the first word, and for any other important word. When you make up a title, try to think of one that will really tell what your writing is about. Try to use a title that is short and interesting.

tongue Your **tongue** is part of your mouth. Your **tongue** helps you to taste food and to speak.

tonight **Tonight** is the night at the end of today. Our family is going out to see a play **tonight**.

too 1. **Too** means also. I had cake, and some ice cream **too**. 2. **Too much** is more than you need. I ate **too much** dessert.

took Dad **took** us to the movies last night. **Took** is a form of the word TAKE.

tool We use **tools** to do work. A saw is a **tool** for cutting wood.

tooth A **tooth** is one of the set of hard, white parts in the mouth. **Teeth** are used for biting and chewing food.

top The **top** is the highest part of something. The roof is the **top** of a building.

touch When you **touch** a thing, you put your hand on it. Carrie **touched** the wet paint and got some on her finger.

toward **Toward** means in the direction of. The boat turned and headed **toward** the shore.

town A **town** is a place where people live and work. A **town** is smaller than a city. **Towns** have buildings, streets, and parks.

toy A **toy** is something a child plays with. Dolls are **toys**.

trade To **trade** is to give one thing for another. Chris **traded** some of his baseball cards for some of Dave's.

traffic All the cars riding on a road are **traffic**. We had to drive home slowly because of the heavy **traffic**.

Traffic on a street in New York City.

train A line of railroad cars pulled by an engine is a **train**. **Trains** move people and things from one place to another.

trash **Trash** is anything that is thrown away and not wanted.

121

travel To **travel** is to go from one place to another. Our family is **traveling** around the country this summer. Someone who **travels** is a **traveler**.

tree A **tree** is a tall woody plant. Birds build their nests in **trees**.

triangle A **triangle** is a shape with three sides, like this. Δ

trip **1.** To **trip** is to hit your foot on something and fall. I **tripped** over a rock as I was running. **2.** To take a **trip** is to go from one place to another. Last week we took a **trip** to the zoo.

trouble **Trouble** is something that causes problems. Jerry got in **trouble** for missing school. Mom is having **trouble** with her car, so she has to get it fixed.

truck A **truck** is a big, strong, heavy car. **Trucks** have a space in back to carry things.

true Something that is **true** is not false or made up. I know that's a **true** story, because I was there and saw the whole thing. If a thing is **true,** it is the **truth.**

trust To **trust** people is to believe what they say and do.

try **1.** To **try** is to work to do something. Henry **tried** to catch the ball, but it was too high and he missed it. **2.** To test something by using it is to **try** it. **Try** this new kind of soup and see if you like it.

Tuesday **Tuesday** is a day of the week. **Tuesday** comes after Monday.

turkey A **turkey** is a large bird with brown feathers. **Turkeys** are eaten as food.

turn To **turn** is to move along in a circle. The wheels of a car **turn** as it goes. You can open a door by **turning** the handle. Matt **turned** his head to watch the girl walk by.

turtle A **turtle** is an animal with a soft body and a hard shell. **Turtles** live on land or in water.

TV **TV** is a short way of saying or writing TELEVISION.

twice **Twice** means two times. Joyce liked the book so much that she read it **twice**.

two **Two** is the word for the number **2**. **Two** is more than one and less than three.

Uu Vv

a b c d e f g h i j k l m n o p q r s t U V w x y z

ugly   Something that is **ugly** is bad to look at. It is not pretty.

umbrella   An **umbrella** is a cover you hold over your head to keep off the rain or sun.

uncle   Your **uncle** is the brother of your mother or your father.

under   If you are **under** a thing, it is above you. My dog likes to lie **under** the kitchen table. "Children **under** 12" means children less than 12 years old.

understand   You **understand** a thing when you know what it means. I **understand** the lesson, now that my teacher went over it with me.
—**understands, understood, understanding.**

unhappy   If you are **unhappy,** you are not happy. You are sad.

uniform   **Uniforms** are special clothes that are all the same. The girls on the 'Red Hots' soccer team wear red **uniforms.**

United States   The **United States of America** is the country that we live in. It is also called the **U. S.** or **U. S. A.** or **America.**

universe   The **universe** is made up of all the planets and stars in space. Everything we see in the sky at night is in the **universe.**

unless   We will go to the park this afternoon, **unless** it rains.

until   **Until** means up to a certain time. Mom said I could stay up **until** nine o'clock tonight.

unusual   If a thing is **unusual,** you don't see it often. White is an **unusual** color for a horse. Very few horses have this color.

123

up   A thing that is **up** is not down. He threw the ball **up** in the air. I stayed **up** until 9:30.

upset   When you are **upset,** you are mad or sad. Benny was **upset** when his sister made fun of his new haircut.

us   Mike and I want to go to the park. Can you give **us** a ride?

use   When you **use** a thing, you do something with it. You **use** a knife to cut things.
—**uses, used, using.**

usual   Something is **usual** if it happens most of the time. The bus **usually** gets here about 7:30.

vacation   A **vacation** is a special time when people do not go to school or work. His family took a week's **vacation** at the beach.

valentine   A **valentine** is a special note you give someone to say you like them. You send **valentines** on **Valentine's Day.**

valley   A **valley** is a low place between two hills or mountains.

vegetable   A **vegetable** is a kind of plant that people eat. Peas and beans are **vegetables.**

very   A lion is a big animal. An elephant is a **very** big animal.

village   A **village** is a small town.

violin   A **violin** makes music. **Violins** have strings.

visit   When you **visit** someone, you go to see the person. I went to **visit** my aunt for a week.

voice   Your **voice** is the sound you make when you talk.

vote   When you **vote,** you say if you want or don't want a thing. In the United States, people **vote** to choose who will be President.

vowel   The letters **a e i o u** are **vowels.** The other letters are **consonants. Y** can be either one.

verbs   Let's say you want to write a story. Here's something to write about: "Katie and I, soccer in the yard, the ball down the hill, I after it." But that's not a story, is it? You have some **nouns,** such as Katie, ball, and hill. **Nouns** name things. But nothing is happening, because there are no verbs. A **verb** shows what happens. It tells what a noun does, or what it is. Here's the same thing with verbs: "Today Katie and I played soccer in the yard. The ball rolled down the hill, and I ran after it."

W w

a b c d e f g h i j k l m n o p q r s t u v **w** x y z

wagon   A **wagon** has four wheels and is used to carry things. Before there were cars or trucks, people carried things in **wagons** pulled by horses.

wait   To **wait** is to stay in a place or do nothing, until someone comes or something happens. We're **waiting** for Dad to come home. Tim **waited** for the bus.

wake   To **wake** means to stop sleeping. Teri likes to **wake** up early in the morning. Please be quiet, or you'll **wake** the baby.

walk   To **walk** means to travel on foot. Maria **walks** to school every day. Sam took his dog for a **walk** on the beach.

wall   A **wall** is one side of a room or building. Cathy hung a picture on her bedroom **wall**. The castle had high stone **walls.**

want   To **want** is to wish you could have or do something. Susan **wants** a new bike. Doug **wanted** to go to the library.

war   A **war** is a long fight between armies. Many soldiers died in our country's **wars.**

warm   Something that is **warm** is a little hot. The weather was so **warm** that I wore shorts to school. The car engine will **warm** up after it runs a while.

was   My cousin **was** in town yesterday. She **was** visiting for the day. **Was** is a form of the word BE. It tells about the past.

wash   To **wash** is to clean with water, or with soap and water. **Wash** your hands before eating. He **washed** the dishes in the sink. A **washing machine** is a thing used for **washing** clothes.

watch **1.** To **watch** is to look at something closely. You **watch** a movie, a play, or a TV show. **2.** A **watch** is a small machine used for telling time.

water **Water** is a liquid that falls from the sky as rain. It makes up the oceans, lakes, and rivers. We use **water** to drink, to wash, and to **water** plants.

Niagara Falls is a famous **waterfall.**

wave **1.** To **wave** your hand means to move it quickly from side to side. We **wave** our hands to say hello or good-bye. **2.** A **wave** is a moving wall of water. Tico loves to go to the beach and ride on the **waves.**

way The **way** you do a thing is how you do it. Take Oak Street. That's the fastest **way** to get downtown. Studying hard is the best **way** to get good grades.

we **We** means the person who is speaking, and others with that person. My family used to live in Ohio. Now **we** live in Texas.

weak **Weak** means not strong. Ernesto was sick for four days, and he still feels **weak** today.

wear When you **wear** a thing, you put it on your body. Janet **wore** her new coat to school. —**wears, wore, worn, wearing.**

weather The **weather** is what the air is like outdoors. Our grass is brown because of the hot, dry **weather** this month.

Wednesday **Wednesday** is a day of the week. **Wednesday** comes after Tuesday and before Thursday.

week A **week** is seven days long. The days of the **week** are Sunday, Monday, Tuesday, Wednesday, Thursday, Friday, and Saturday. The **weekend** is the time at the end of the **week** when schools are not open.

weigh To **weigh** a thing is to find out how heavy it is. He **weighed** the bag of apples. It **weighs** 50 pounds. The **weight** of a thing is what it **weighs.**

well   "She's a very <u>good</u> singer. She sings really <u>well</u>." The two words <u>good</u> and <u>well</u> mean the same thing here. How then are they different? <u>Good</u> is used with a noun, <u>singer</u>. (A <u>singer</u> is a person.) <u>Well</u> is used with a verb, <u>sings</u>. (<u>Sings</u> tells what a person does.) <u>Good</u> is an **adjective**. An **adjective** goes with a noun to tell more about it. <u>Well</u> is an **adverb**. An **adverb** goes with a verb to tells more about it. Notice the <u>adverbs</u> in these sentences: He walked <u>slowly</u>. She learns <u>quickly</u>.

well   **Well** means in a good way. Sally plays the piano **well**.

went   **Went** is a form of the word GO. Dennis **went** to the store to buy some milk.

were   **Were** is a form of the word BE. Last week they **were** away, but now they're home.

we're   **We're** is a shorter way to say or write WE ARE. Today **we're** going on a trip to the zoo.

west   **West** is a direction on the earth. You face **west** when you watch the sun go down.

wet   **Wet** means not dry. I hung my **wet** clothes out to dry.

whale   **Whales** are the largest animals in the ocean. A **whale** looks like a huge fish.

what   **What** is her name? **What** school does she go to? I didn't hear you. **What** did you say?

whatever   Dad said we could choose **whatever** we want for lunch at the restaurant.

wheat   **Wheat** is a kind of grass used as food. The tiny grains of **wheat** are used to make **flour,** bread, and other foods.

wheel   A **wheel** is something round that turns to help things move. A bicycle has two **wheels**. A car has four **wheels.**

when   **When** means at what time. **When** does school start? He knows **when** to speak up and **when** to keep quiet.

where   **Where** means in what place. **Where** do you live? Mary forgot **where** she put her coat.

whether   Let us know **whether** you can come or not. You must decide **whether** to stay or go.

which   **Which** means what one. **Which** desk is yours?

while 1. A **while** is a short time. I can only visit for a little **while**. I have to go home soon.
2. **While** means during the time. Billy called for you **while** you were at the store.

white **White** is the lightest of all colors. **White** is the color of milk or snow.

who **Who** means which person. **Who** is that boy there? That's the boy **who** lives next door to me.

whoever **Whoever** means any person who, or the person who. The party is for everyone. **Whoever** wants to, can come.

whole If you have all of a thing, you have the **whole** thing. Our **whole** family went for a walk together. Steven ate a **whole** pie.

who's **Who's** is a shorter way to say or write WHO IS or WHO HAS. **Who's** that on the phone? **Who's** been eating all the cake?

whose **Whose** is a form of the word WHO. "**Whose** house is that?" means "Who owns that house?"

why **Why** means for what reason. **Why** wasn't Ronnie in school today? Peg asked **why** she had to go to bed so early.

wide 1. **Wide** means a long way across. A **wide** river runs past our town.
2. **Wide** also means a certain distance from one side to the other. My room is 15 feet **wide**.

wife A **wife** is a married woman. Husbands and **wives** are married to each other.

wild Something **wild** is not under control. A wolf is a **wild** animal. Dogs are **tame** animals.

will **Will** is used to show that a thing should happen. Leslie **will** be here soon. Dad said, "You **will** clean up your room now!" (See the box on this page.)

will When we talk or write, we use different words to show different times. "It is <u>raining</u> out." (The time is right now.) "It <u>rained</u> last night." (The time is before now.) "The radio said it <u>will rain</u> tomorrow." (The time is yet to come.) The time that is here right now is called the **present**. The time before now is the **past**. The time that has not come yet is the **future**. To tell about the future, we can use either **will** or **going to:** "It looks like it's <u>going to</u> rain. <u>I'll</u> (I <u>will</u>) close the windows."

128

win   To **win** is to be the best in a game or contest. Our team is **winning** the football game.

wind   **Wind** is air that moves over the earth. Strong **winds** often blow during a storm.

This **windmill** uses **wind** power to pump water for a farm in Holland.

window   A **window** is an open area in a wall. **Windows** are made of glass. **Windows** let light and air into a building.

wing   A **wing** is part of a plane or an animal's body that is used for flying. The jet plane had engines on each of its **wings**.

winter   **Winter** comes after fall and before spring. **Winter** is the coldest season of the year.

wire   A **wire** is a long, thin piece of metal that can be bent easily. Different kinds of **wire** are used to carry electricity, to tie things together, and to make fences.

wise   A **wise** person knows about many things and can think carefully. The judge is a very **wise** person.

wish   To **wish** means to want something. Jake **wished** he had a dog. I can't help **wishing** that summer would come.

witch   A **witch** is a make-believe person who has magic powers. Kate and Jan dressed up as **witches** on Halloween.

with   Donna went to the beach **with** her friend Robin. The dog was covered **with** mud. Mom has been having trouble **with** her car.

within   **Within** means inside of. We have to finish the test **within** one hour.

without   **Without** means not having or doing. Mike asked for a hamburger **without** any roll. Dad was in such a hurry that he left **without** eating breakfast.

woke I **woke** up at six o'clock this morning. **Woke** is a form of the word WAKE.

wolf A **wolf** is a wild animal that looks like a dog. A **wolf** has gray fur and a long tail. **Wolves** live in the forest.

This is called a **gray wolf** or **timber wolf.**

woman When a girl grows up, she's called a **woman.** Mom is at lunch with two other **women.**

won Our team **won** the game yesterday. **Won** is a form of the word WIN.

wonder To **wonder** is to want to know about something. Charles **wondered** how many stars are in the sky. I **wonder** why our dog hasn't come home yet.

wonderful When something is **wonderful**, it's very, very good. We had a **wonderful** time on our summer vacation.

won't **Won't** is a shorter way to say or write WILL NOT. Sally's sick, so she **won't** be able to go.

wood **Wood** comes from trees. **Wood** can be cut and burned in a fire, or used to build houses, furniture, and other things.

wool **Wool** is the thick, curly hair of sheep. It is used to make clothing, rugs, and blankets.

word We use **words** to talk and speak. This book tells you about **words.** "Cat" is a **word.** "Czt" is not a **word.** It has no meaning.

wore Sherry **wore** her new dress to school yesterday. **Wore** is a form of the word WEAR.

work 1. Using your body or mind to do something is **work.** Cutting wood is hard **work.** Tim **worked** all day on his report. 2. **Work** is a job. She just left for **work.** She **works** as a doctor.

world The **world** is the place where all people live. It is another name for the Earth.

worry   To **worry** is to feel that something bad may happen. Vicky is **worried** that she won't do well on the test. She's been **worrying** about it all week.

worse   **Worse** and **worst** are forms of the word BAD. The weather was bad last month, but it's even **worse** now. It's the **worst** winter we've had here in ten years.

worth   **1.** How much something costs is how much it is **worth.** Mom bought ten dollars **worth** of gas. A thing that is not **worth** anything is **worthless.**
2. Worth also means good enough for. This toy is broken. It's not **worth** keeping.

would   **Would** is a form of the word WILL. When I was little, my parents **would** often take me to the park to play. **Would** you like some orange juice?

wrap   When a thing is **wrapped,** it is covered with something else. She's going to **wrap** the birthday present in bright red **wrapping** paper.

write   To **write** means to make letters and words on paper. Jane likes to **write** with a blue pen. John **wrote** a report about tigers for school. A person who writes a book or story is called a **writer.** —writes, wrote, written, writing.

writing   **1.** Putting words on paper is called **writing.** (See the box on this page.)
2. Something written is also called **writing.** The teacher told me I have nice, neat **writing.**

wrong   **Wrong** means not right. He had only one **wrong** answer on the test. It is **wrong** to tell a lie. We got to the game at the **wrong** time. It was already over.

---

writing   Here are some ways to help yourself become a better writer.
    Read. People who became famous writers grew up in different ways. Some lived on farms, and some lived in big cities. Some were poor, and others were not. But these writers were all alike in one way. They all read a lot when they were young. You can learn to <u>write</u> by <u>reading</u> what other have written.
    Write. These famous writers practiced writing all the time. They kept a diary or a journal, and they wrote papers for school.
    Look and Listen. Writers are careful to notice what is around them. They remember what a place looks like, and what sounds it has.

x-ray An **x-ray** is a picture that shows the inside of something. **X-rays** are used to take pictures of bones and other parts inside the body.

yard A **yard** is an area of grass or open land near a house. That house has a big back **yard**.

yard A **yard** is a way to measure how long something is. A **yard** is 36 inches long. It is the same as three feet.

yawn **Yawn** means to open your mouth wide and take in air. People may **yawn** if they are tired.

year A **year** is an amount of time. A **year** is the same as 12 months, or 365 days. My baby sister is two **years** old.

yellow **Yellow** is a bright color. Lemons and bananas have **yellow** skin. If a girl has **yellow** hair, we say she is a **blonde.**

yes When you say **yes**, you want something to happen or you think it is right. Mom said '**yes**' when I asked if I could sleep over at my friend's house. **Yes**, you have the right answer to the question.

yesterday The day before today was **yesterday**. **Yesterday** I was six years old. Today is my birthday, and now I'm seven.

yet When we are waiting for something to happen, we ask if it has happened **yet**. Donna wanted to know if it was time to leave **yet**. Did you finish your homework **yet**?

you Let's say a girl named Cathy Moore is talking to her friend Rose Garcia. She wants to ask her something. "Cathy Moore wants to ask Rose Garcia a question. Do Cathy and Rose and the rest of the class have a test today?" People don't really talk that way, though. Cathy would just say, **"I** want to ask **you** a question" and "Do **we** have a test today?" Words like <u>I</u>, <u>you</u>, or <u>we</u> are called **pronouns**. A **pronoun** can be used to take the place of a <u>noun</u>.

you Someone who is talking to another person uses the word **you**. **You** are reading this book. Eddie called me up and asked, "Can **you** come out and play?" (See the box on this page.)

young A person who is not very old is **young**. Children are **young** people. Kittens are **young** cats.

your If you have a dog, it is **your** dog. I'll tell Mike that you called—what is **your** name?

yours A thing that you own or have is **yours**. This pencil is **yours,** and that one is mine.

yourself If you do a thing, you do it **yourself**. Did you hurt **yourself** when you fell? Give me a cookie and take one for **yourself.**

zebra A **zebra** is an animal. **Zebras** are white with black stripes. They look like horses.

zero When there is nothing, it is **zero**. If you take away four from four, the answer is **zero**. The number for **zero** is **0.**

zipper A **zipper** is a thing that holds two parts of clothes together. **Zippers** are long and are made of metal or plastic.

zoo A **zoo** is a place where people can see wild animals. **Zoos** have many kinds of wild animals, such as lions, tigers, bears, elephants, and monkeys.

The **zebra's** stripes make it hard to see.

INDEX

This Index lists all the Language Features that are found in the dictionary. Some of the items in the Index are in dark print, **like this.** When you see an item in dark print, it means that this item is the name of one of the Language Features. Other items appear in regular print. This means that the item is talked about in a Language Feature on the page shown. When there are other listings indented under a main heading, this means that the idea is further discussed under those additional items.